MABEL CHEUNG YUEN-TING'S
An Autumn's Tale

Hong Kong University Press thanks Xu Bing for writing the Press's name in his Square Word Calligraphy for the covers of its books. For further information see p. iv.

THE NEW HONG KONG CINEMA SERIES

The New Hong Kong Cinema came into existence under very special circumstances, during a period of social and political crisis resulting in a change of cultural paradigms. Such critical moments have produced the cinematic achievements of the early Soviet cinema, neorealism, the *nouvelle vague*, and the German cinema of the 1970s and, we can now say, the New Hong Kong Cinema. If this cinema grew increasingly intriguing in the 1980s, after the announcement of Hong Kong's return to China, it is largely because it had to confront a new cultural and political space that was both complex and hard to define, where the problems of colonialism were uncannily overlaid with those of globalism. Such uncanniness could not be caught through straight documentary or conventional history writing: it was left to the cinema to define it.

Has the creative period of the New Hong Kong Cinema now come to an end? However we answer the question, there is a need to evaluate the achievements of Hong Kong cinema. This series distinguishes itself from the other books on the subject by focusing in-depth on individual Hong Kong films, which together make the New Hong Kong Cinema.

Series General Editors
Ackbar Abbas, Wimal Dissanayake, Mette Hjort, Gina Marchetti, Stephen Teo

Series Advisors
Chris Berry, Nick Browne, Ann Hui, Leo Lee, Li Cheuk-to, Patricia Mellencamp, Meaghan Morris, Paul Willemen, Peter Wollen, Wu Hung

Other titles in the series

Andrew Lau and Alan Mak's *Infernal Affairs – The Trilogy* by Gina Marchetti

Fruit Chan's *Durian Durian* by Wendy Gan

John Woo's *A Better Tomorrow* by Karen Fang

King Hu's *A Touch of Zen* by Stephen Teo

Stanley Kwan's *Center Stage* by Mette Hjort

Tsui Hark's *Zu: Warriors From the Magic Mountain* by Andrew Schroeder

Wong Kar-wai's *Ashes of Time* by Wimal Dissanayake

Wong Kar-wai's *Happy Together* by Jeremy Tambling

MABEL CHEUNG YUEN-TING'S
An Autumn's Tale

Stacilee Ford

香港大學出版社
HONG KONG UNIVERSITY PRESS

Hong Kong University Press
14/F Hing Wai Centre
7 Tin Wan Praya Road
Aberdeen
Hong Kong

ISBN 978-962-209-894-7

British Library Cataloguing-in-Publication Data
A catalogue record for this book is available from the British Library.

Secure on-line Ordering
http://www.hkupress.org

Printed and bound by Liang Yu Printing Fty. Ltd., Hong Kong, China

Hong Kong University Press is honoured that Xu Bing, whose
art explores the complex themes of language across cultures,
has written the Press's name in his Square Word Calligraphy.
This signals our commitment to cross-cultural thinking and the
distinctive nature of our English-language books published in
China.

"At first glance, Square Word Calligraphy appears to be nothing
more unusual than Chinese characters, but in fact it is a new
way of rendering English words in the format of a square so they
resemble Chinese characters. Chinese viewers expect to be able
to read Square Word Calligraphy but cannot. Western viewers,
however are surprised to find they can read it. Delight erupts
when meaning is unexpectedly revealed."
— Britta Erickson, *The Art of Xu Bing*

Contents

Series Preface

The New Hong Kong cinema came into existence under very special circumstances, during a period of social and political crisis resulting in a change of cultural paradigms. Such critical moments have produced the cinematic achievements of the early Soviet cinema, neorealism, the *nouvelle vague*, the German cinema in the 1970s and, we can now say, the recent Hong Kong cinema. If this cinema grew increasingly intriguing in the 1980s, after the announcement of Hong Kong's return to China, it was largely because it had to confront a new cultural and political space that was both complex and hard to define, where the problems of colonialism were overlaid with those of globalism in an uncanny way. Such uncanniness could not be caught through straight documentary or conventional history writing; it was left to the cinema to define it.

It does so by presenting to us an urban space that slips away if we try to grasp it too directly, a space that cinema coaxes into existence by whatever means at its disposal. Thus it is by eschewing a narrow idea of relevance and pursuing disreputable genres like melodrama, kung fu and the fantastic that cinema brings into view something else about the city which could otherwise be missed. One classic example is Stanley Kwan's *Rouge*, which draws on the unrealistic form of the ghost story to evoke something of the uncanniness of Hong Kong's urban space. It takes a ghost to catch a ghost.

In the new Hong Kong cinema, then, it is neither the subject matter nor a particular set of generic conventions that is paramount. In fact, many Hong Kong films begin by following generic conventions but proceed to transform them. Such transformation of genre is also the transformation of a sense of place where all the rules have quietly and deceptively changed. It is this shifting sense of place, often expressed negatively and indirectly — but in the best work always rendered precisely in (necessarily) innovative images — that is decisive for the New Hong Kong Cinema.

Has the creative period of the New Hong Kong Cinema come to an end? However we answer the question, there is a need now to evaluate the achievements of Hong Kong cinema. During the last few years, a number of full-length books have appeared, testifying to the topicality of the subject. These books survey the field with varying degrees of success, but there is yet an almost complete lack of authoritative texts focusing in depth on individual Hong Kong films. This book series on the New Hong Kong Cinema is designed to fill this lack. Each volume will be written by a scholar/critic who will analyse each chosen film in detail and provide a critical apparatus for further discussion including filmography and bibliography.

Our objective is to produce a set of interactional and provocative readings that would make a self-aware intervention into modern Hong Kong culture. We advocate no one theoretical position; the authors will approach their chosen films from their own distinct points of vantage and interest. The aim of the series is to generate open-ended discussions of the selected films, employing diverse analytical strategies, in order to urge the readers towards self-reflective engagements with the films in particular and the Hong Kong cultural space in general. It is our hope that this series will contribute to the sharpening of Hong Kong culture's conceptions of itself.

In keeping with our conviction that film is not a self-enclosed signification system but an important cultural practice among similar others, we wish to explore how films both reflect and inflect culture. And it is useful to keep in mind that reflection of reality and reality of reflection are equally important in the understanding of cinema.

Ackbar Abbas
Wimal Dissanayake

Preface to *An Autumn's Tale*

An Autumn's Tale quietly reaches out to the Hong Kong film fan open to a change of pace from martial arts capers, police dramas, and Chinese historical epics. A diasporic romance featuring subtle but powerful performances by lead actors Chow Yun Fat and Cherie Chung, the film offers a refreshing glimpse of how people are changed by the cross-cultural encounter. Released in 1987, and directed by Mabel Cheung Yuen-ting, An *Autumn's Tale* is the first film made by a woman director to be featured in this series. Cheung, one of Hong Kong's well-known Second Wave directors, and her partner and husband Alex Law (who wrote the screenplay), capture a particular moment in the histories of both Hong Kong and the U.S. The characters in the film live in the Chinatown area of New York City in the late 1980s where many Hong Kong people made second homes, and became "Americanized" to varying degrees as they sought opportunity (and a second passport) prior to the resumption of Chinese (PRC) sovereignty in 1997.

Simultaneously claiming and contesting canonical myths of immigrant acculturation and the American dream, *An Autumn's Tale* is, in many respects, a transnational American studies text, offering up a contemporary take on immigration, multiculturalism, and romance in diaspora. Cheung spotlights the increasing interdependence between the people and histories of China and the United States. The film challenges Hollywood stereotypes of the Chinese diaspora and of Chinese Americans as inscrutable or exotic. It also offers a counter narrative to Eurocentric representations of immigrant success and acculturation to American society. A New York City story set during the Reagan years, the film hints at how post-1965 "new immigration" was changing New York even as the city struggled to pull itself out of economic depression. If, as Kwai-Cheung Lo notes, "Popular culture is a kind of empowering force for the diasporic Hong Kong Chinese in foreign environments," *An Autumn's Tale* offers several paths to empowerment through romance and fantasy. On a somewhat more autobiographical level, the film is connected to Cheung's actual experiences as a graduate student at New York University. Because of her own familiarity with both the U.S. and Hong Kong, *An Autumn's Tale* offers an insider/outsider take on what it means to "make it" in America in the late 20th century.[1]

Drawing on scholarship in several domains in addition to transnational American studies, such as gender studies, Asian American studies and Hong Kong cultural studies, this discussion of *An Autumn's Tale* will argue that the cinematic representations presented in the film reflect a point of view that both engages with and talks back to histories, myths, and core cultural values in the U.S. In some ways, the film resembles examples of Asian American cultural production which perform (to borrow Lisa Lowe's term) "Immigrant Acts," yet the Hong Kong connection adds a unique dimension. *An Autumn's Tale* is both familiar (and it reveals how Hong Kong people share in the historical experience of the U.S.)

yet it is still marked by a certain "foreign-ness." Read against Hollywood representations of Asia and its cultures which, to this day, construct Chinese people as "other" — exotic, brainy, inscrutable or comic caricatures — *An Autumn's Tale,* like several other Hong Kong films made during this period, shatters the aforementioned stereotypes and offers examples of "other modes of retrieving and spatializing history."[2] As it does so, the film suggests new ways to think about those who are recent arrivals in the U.S. as well as those who have been Americans for generations. *An Autumn's Tale* is a film that engages in border crossing between Hong Kong and the U.S. and this study crosses borders between film traditions and disciplinary perspectives in order to illuminate the themes and preoccupations present in *An Autumn's Tale.* The film is a quiet but important intervention into a cinematic and cultural conversation about Chinese and American identities. It also raises — albeit in a light-hearted manner — multiple issues about cultural adjustment, gender, romance, and urban life at the end of the 20th century when the movement of people, culture, and capital quickened and changed both Asia and the United States in profound ways. While the aesthetic and technical aspects of *An Autumn's Tale* will be considered here, the main purpose of this study is to discuss the film as a cultural history text. Considering it in this light paves the way for further discussion of non-American popular culture texts within the domain of cultural and transnational American studies.

Acknowledgements

First and foremost, I extend sincere thanks to Gina Marchetti, who graciously reaches across disciplinary boundaries and looks for ways to enrich the conversation about Hong Kong film in many settings. She suggested I consider writing for the series and I have been the beneficiary of her formidable knowledge of film. It has been a pleasure to work with Colin Day and Ian Lok at Hong Kong University Press. Colin's commitment to Hong Kong cultural studies is evident in the way he inspires his authors. Ian's efficiency and patience with me was extraordinary. I thank Phoebe Chan and Dennis Cheung for offering their expertise in the final phases of production. A thorough reading of the manuscript by Christina Klein helped focus and improve the study. I appreciate her attention to the larger themes as well as the small details. At several points during the process of writing about *An Autumn's Tale* I was lucky enough to have lively conversations with the director of the film, Mabel Cheung Yuen-ting and the writer of the screenplay, Alex Law. In their professional and personal lives they exemplify true partnership. *An Autumn's Tale* is their gift to Hong Kong film fans. Their willingness to share their time and reflections two decades after the film's release was a gift to me.

For comments on early drafts and paper presentations I thank Evelyn Ng, Karen Jo Laidler, Gary McDonogh, Cindy Wong, and Patricia Chiu. Gordon Slethaug and Geetanjali Singh are dear friends and colleagues who taught me how to practice transnational American studies. This book is one of several projects growing out of years of happy collaboration with both of them and the students, visiting scholars, and teaching colleagues who have been part of the American Studies team at the University of Hong Kong. Thanks to my colleagues in the Department of History who understand the importance of cultural history, particularly Peter Cunich, Maureen Sabine, Tom Stanley, David Pomfret, Marie-Paul Ha, and Priscilla Roberts. Lily Lew watched the film with me and shared her own impressions of *An Autumn's Tale* as well as helping me understand the Cantonese slang that flew by me. For several years she has helped me think more clearly and honestly about a number of issues, professional and personal. I am grateful for her insights and clarity. Taunalyn Rutherford offered valuable feedback after I presented a paper on *An Autumn's Tale* at the American Studies Association meeting during the late stages of writing.

Finally, heartfelt thanks to my father, Leland Ford, and my mother, the late Denece Ford, for passing along a love of movies and the conversations they generate. To Matthew, Tyler, and Ian Hosford — who helped me make a home in Hong Kong — I express my gratitude for their good humor and patience. I look forward to sharing movies — and more — with them in the years to come.

Introduction
Mabel Cheung Yuen-ting and the Women of Hong Kong's Second Wave

Despite the fact that Mabel Cheung Yuen-ting is the first woman director to be recognized in this series, she and her peers have had a significant impact on the Hong Kong film industry. Scholars who have noted that the 1980s was a golden decade for Hong Kong film, also remind us that women's cultural production in Hong Kong accelerated in the last two decades of the 20th century. Directors such as Cheung rode a wave of increased profile and popularity.[1] One of three women to achieve acclaim in the New Wave/Second Wave cohort — along with Ann Hui and Clara Law — Mabel Chueng Yuen-ting's work speaks to multiple preoccupations in diaspora, while making a woman's story — through the character of Jenny (played by Cherie Chung) — the central focus. *An Autumn's Tale* is a piece of women's history (in terms of both its content and its production) and it is also an important example of how the Hong Kong film industry (particularly in the 1980s and 1990s) chronicled the diversity of women's experiences, changes in ideas about gender identities, class cleavages, and transpacific migration at century's end. The film complements and is in conversation with other Hong Kong films about women in diaspora made during the same period such as Allen Fong's *Just Like Weather* (1986), Stanley Kwan's *Full Moon in New York* (1987), Ann Hui's *Song of the Exile* (1989), Clara Law's *Farewell China* (1990) and *A Floating Life* (1996), and Evans Chan's *Crossings* (1994).

Cheung, Hui, and Law do more than tell women's stories. They all make films that address multiple issues and historical shifts in gender, ethnic, and cultural identities. In some respects, several of their films could be considered a transnational extension of an Asian American cultural studies tradition; a late-20th century accompaniment to the 19th century "bachelor society" narratives of men who left Hong Kong and China to work and live in the United States during the Gold Rush period. Hong Kong's 1980s and 1990s cinematic migration melodramas like *An Autumn's Tale* also merit closer analysis for the counter narrative their representations offer in a particular historical moment. Recently, increased interest in Chinese women's autobiographical texts (particularly stories of women from the Chinese mainland during and after the Cultural Revolution) has extended a long-standing western proclivity to view Chinese women everywhere as tragic victims. Films like *An Autumn's Tale* offer a different perspective on the story of women coming of age. They are, arguably, cultural history texts that show women exercising a significant amount of agency through mobility, education, and acculturation to various environments. Gender and cultural identity are important, but by no means the defining factors in shaping women's lives.

Because this is the first study of a female director in the Hong Kong New Wave Cinema series, it is important to take a brief step back in order to assess the status of women in the Hong Kong film industry. How difficult is it for women to succeed? Cheung declares she feels "lucky to be a female director in Hong Kong" because, "in all of Asia, Hong Kong is the place which has the least prejudice against women." All that really matters, she notes, is whether a director can bring a film in on time and under budget. [2] Actor and director Tsui Hark proudly declares that the presence of strong women behind and in front of the camera is one thing that makes Hong Kong different from Hollywood. "In Hong Kong, we are never 'threatened' by the females in our films and there is no bias in choosing which gender is doing the interesting things in the story."[3]

Yet while she stands firmly behind the declaration that being a woman is not a liability for a director, Cheung is pleased that several recent changes have taken place, particularly in terms of women in front of the camera. She is, she says, happy that "the depiction of women in Hong Kong movies has evolved from mere decoration for the set to characters with independent thinking."[4] Keep in mind, however, that despite the confident declarations of an increasingly level playing field, women are still significantly outnumbered in the industry and Cheung was one of only a select few women directors when *An Autumn's Tale* was released in 1987. Public utterances to the contrary, Cheung and other women in the industry have had to make their way in a particularly male-dominated space.

Cheung's background and education prepared her well for the type of border crossing that takes place in her films. Following her graduation from the University of Hong Kong, she studied drama and writing at the University of Bristol. She worked as a producer at Radio/Television Hong Kong (RTHK) between 1978 and 1980 before going to New York University where she studied filmmaking from 1980 to 1983.[5] This broad exposure to overseas film industries is typical of a cadre of Hong Kong filmmakers. Many spent a portion of their early careers working in television in Hong Kong as well as studying at film schools in the United States and/or in Britain. Several continue to move between Hong Kong and other large cities throughout the world. Labeled the "Second Wave," because they came after Hong Kong's New Wave directors, members of this cohort include Cheung, Law, Eddie Fong, Clara Law, Lawrence Ah

Mon, Stanley Kwan, Jacob Cheung, Evans Chan, Ching Siu-ting, and Wong Kar-wai. Many of these directors are known for "innovative artistic styles but also their new perspectives in approaching history and gender/sexuality issues."[6] While speaking of Stanley Kwan's films, Cui Shuqin's insight is applicable to Cheung and other Second-Wave directors. Cui notes that the "orientation of Kwan's cinema towards the feminine and its place in a moment of historical transition calls attention to the relatedness of Hong Kong, gender, and history." As such, his films "situate women as intrinsic to the development of new postmodern modes of speaking and writing."[7] Like Kwan, all of these directors feature strong, complex women in their films and they offer intricate plots, nuanced characterizations, and settings dealing with sexuality, gender bending, and the tension between cultural expectations and personal desires.

Cheung and her Second Wave peers stepped into the spotlight at a propitious time. As Law Kar and Frank Ben have written, "the years between 1983 and 1993 were, in fact, a glorious golden period with unprecedented achievement in quality, quantity, and market success."[8] Although there are a number of possible reasons for this creative burst of energy, Hong Kong's return to Chinese sovereignty provided one source of inspiration. Cheung and her second-wave peers belong to a generation that lived through the late-colonial era and the transition to Chinese sovereignty. Many Hong Kong film scholars have noted the importance of the period between the signing of the Sino-British Joint Declaration in 1984 and the transition to PRC control in 1997. Stephen Teo asserts that "the second half of the 80s was possibly the most interesting period of Hong Kong cinema," partly because of the preoccupation with 1997.[9]

Teo argues that Second Wave directors are different from their New Wave predecessors in that their stance towards 1997 is more introspective and less cynical.[10] This is certainly the case with *An*

Autumn's Tale which shines an almost fairy-tale-like light on relations between various sub-ethnic Chinese populations in New York, and suggests no hint of anxiety about the pending transition to PRC sovereignty in Hong Kong. The audience sees that Jenny is comfortable either in Hong Kong or in the U.S. but that her opportunities for self-determination seem to be more plentiful outside of Hong Kong. In fact, Jenny's cinematic adjustment to life in New York City is based to a significant extent on Cheung and Law's experiences as graduate students there in the 1980s. Because the film was made prior to the events of June 1989 in Beijing, when viewed today, *An Autumn's Tale* reflects a certain pre-Tiananmen Square optimism. It is, in some respects, a historical document offering an idealistic blueprint for transnational bonding among those who wish to claim a pan-Chinese ethnic identity.

Cheung is not the only Hong Kong director whose work reflects ties to actual autobiographical events. Comparing Cheung, Ann Hui and Clara Law, Gina Marchetti has pointed out that all three share common ground in their educational background, "choice of genres, thematic preoccupations, and aesthetic interests." All studied film in the United States or the United Kingdom (Cheung spent time in the U.K. as well.), worked at Radio/Television Hong Kong (RTHK) before becoming film directors, and are "comfortable with multilingual productions and subjects that cross national borders." Marchetti adds that all three have "a preoccupation with themes of exile, nomadism, migration, split/multiple/uncertain identities and intergenerational conflict ... Each has used her experiences living abroad as the basis for films on emigration from Hong Kong."[11] Another preoccupation evident in these films is the drive to define what it means to be a Hong Kong person. Like others belonging to a generation of Hong Kong youth who saw themselves as distinct from (and more westernized than) their Mainland cousins, it seems that Cheung and her cohort have the option of negotiating various identity dilemmas through their cinematic works.

Discussions of Hong Kong identity are, in these films, coupled to debates about gender and civil society in Hong Kong in the final years of the colonial period. The 1980s was a decade of consciousness raising and coalition building for a burgeoning women's movement in Hong Kong and many women's groups were formed or strengthened. As Eliza Lee notes, "Colonial resistance, reflection on one's Chinese identity, and the formation of a local Hong Kong identity were thus integral to the postcolonial subjectivity. In this sense, the rise of an indigenous women's movement in the 1980s was part of the post-coloniality."[12] The 1980s were not a time of profound legislative gain (significant change came in the 1990s when CEDAW — the Convention to Eliminate Discrimination Against Women — and the Sex Discrimination Ordinance were passed and the Equal Opportunities Commission formed). However, the period did see a certain feminist ferment, and Hong Kong films like *An Autumn's Tale* and others made in this period open a window revealing shifting attitudes about changes in women's lives, as well as in Hong Kong society more generally.

Because Cheung and other women who transited between Hong Kong and "the west" became comfortable in more than one environment, migration melodramas are, arguably, a forum for and an opportunity to enter the lively transnational conversation about women, migration, and success — personally and professionally. As feminist cultural studies scholars have noted, films do important "cultural work" as they explore the processes of embracing or eschewing social change. Cinema has been a particularly important cultural and historical text in Hong Kong. It offers a vehicle for discussing and pushing against the grain of Hong Kong's unique history as a British Colony under the influence of rather conservative and authoritarian ideas about women, their place in society, and gender identities emanating from colonial leaders and more local neo-Confucian, as well as capitalist, orthodoxies.

"Despite the emergence of a nascent, albeit vibrant, local feminist movement in the 1980s and 1990s," Lisa Fischler writes, "patriarchal aspects of local politics, such as conservative views of women's familial roles and responsibilities and of their presence in the public sphere, made up a substantial part of the institutions and practices limiting women activists' construction of a strong, public feminist agenda."[13]

An Autumn's Tale explores how women can follow new paths and seek self-fulfillment. In fact, many Hong Kong film melodramas released during this period reflect views similar to those noted by Fischler as well as a palatable ambivalence about women's push for equality. On one hand, women were encouraged to "uphold Asian values" (be filial, respect Confucian mores, and avoid conflict) and protect the family from the excesses of the free market in Hong Kong. Yet at the same time, women were also told it was vital that they pursue independence by gaining an education and seeking employment, thus supplementing family incomes and bolstering the Hong Kong economy. In the attention it pays to the woman in diaspora, *An Autumn's Tale* prepares women for the mixed signals they will receive in contemporary society — at home or abroad. It is one of many films about Hong Kong women "sorting themselves out" in various locations, but in this case, the setting is New York. Gina Marchetti, Elaine Ho, and Geetanjali Singh have noted the importance of looking at Hong Kong women's narratives of negotiation with modernity in order to understand shifting currents of gender, postcoloniality, culture, and socio-economic change.[14] They argue that Hong Kong women must forge identities in the face of multiple and conflicting demands linked to both western and Chinese cultural traditions. As the audience sees Jenny finding her way in New York, she models possible alternatives for young women envisioning their own paths to individuation amid external influences including familial and cultural expectations.

The negotiation continues today on both sides of the Pacific. Women who enjoy economic success and public notoriety can be perceived as a threat anywhere, but in Hong Kong society, for a woman to be seen as unfeminine or overbearing (despite the fact that she may be powerful and articulate) is to risk alienation from family, peers, and business associates. Harmony is prized above all and feminism (particularly in its American form) has a reputation in Hong Kong for being anything but harmonious.[15] Still, the impact of a women's movement that is global — not just western — in its reach, manifests itself in Hong Kong. Women who left and then returned to Hong Kong, like Cheung and her sister directors, made films that explored new paths for both women and men. As Siumi Maria Tam and others have shown, for women, "emigration from Hong Kong introduced an experience of 'empowering mobility' despite the stresses of leaving home."[16] In fact, Hong Kong women directors comment that they can and often do challenge gender orthodoxy in the city and in their profession. Yeeshan Chan notes that directors such as Mabel Cheung Yuen-ting and Sylvia Chang "appear to be gentle women," but "they can talk forcefully and humorously at work, using 'masculine' language." Noting that Ann Hui has declared that 'being 'unfeminine' is her advantage in the industry," Chan writes that, "a woman who can free herself from typical feminine characteristics can also free her male co-workers from giving her extra consideration by making them see her as an androgynous colleague."[17]

It is not clear how much of the film's success is due to its discussion of contemporary issues, particularly those linked to women and gender, nor is it possible to assess the impact of the film on women's lives. Still, *An Autumn's Tale* was a commercial success both at home and among diasporic audiences throughout the world. Although some critics point to the box office returns enjoyed by Cheung and others of the Second Wave cohort as evidence that their work is less experimental or artistic than the

New Wave, Second Wave films reached a wider, more global audience.[18] In addition to its popularity among fans in Hong Kong and abroad, *An Autumn's Tale* earned critical favor. Despite its modest budget, it received several honors including 1987 Hong Kong Film Awards for best picture, screenplay, and cinematography, and Chow Yun Fat won a Golden Horse Award for best actor. The most acclaimed of her films, *An Autumn's Tale*'s success came as a surprise to Cheung, her husband and screenwriter Alex Law, and many others. Part of the film's appeal was linked to the fact that Chow Yun Fat played the male lead character, Figgy (the literal translation in Cantonese is Boathead although Figgy is used in the English subtitling of the film). Released approximately one year after the premiere of his breakout film *A Better Tomorrow*, Chow had become an international star by the time *An Autumn's Tale* reached theatres. The diasporic romance was a dramatic departure from the John Woo heroic bloodshed film that most Hong Kong film fans associated with Chow. As such it is a rich text to analyze for its messages about culture and masculinity as well as femininity, both of which are the subject of discussion later in this study.

In addition to the popularity of Chow Yun Fat (and his co-star Cherie Chung, whose career took off in the 1980s), another reason for *An Autumn's Tale*'s success was its appeal to individuals within the Chinese Diaspora hungry for migration stories. As Peter Feng notes, "While Hollywood often traveled to Asia, only rarely did Hollywood films depict Asians who had ventured to America."[19] Audiences could relate to a movie that looked and felt like a Hollywood romance but also discussed (in a light-hearted manner) the complexities of life in the U.S. for recent arrivals from Hong Kong and elsewhere in Asia. Invoking both a Hollywood and a Hong Kong "Home," *An Autumn's Tale,* like several Hong Kong films, served a dual purpose. As scholars have noted, many Hong Kong filmmakers not only live and work in both places — the U.S.

and Hong Kong — they also have a well-established relationship with Hollywood on many levels.[20] In Hong Kong, as Esther Cheung and Chu Yiu-wai remind us, "Hollywood film is more like a model and partner than an 'other' to be resisted, deconstructed, and repelled. Hong Kong cinema indeed is part of Hollywood's hegemony."[21] As Law Kar and Frank Bren have shown in their studies of early Hong Kong cinema, links between the U.S. and Hong Kong are decades old. Actors, directors, and film companies have shared (or swiped) personnel, techniques, and scripts since the early 20th century.[22] However, these cross-cultural connections multiplied more dramatically once the "astronaut" population (individuals who flew back and forth between Hong Kong and second homes in cities throughout the world) began to grow in the 1970s and 1980s. [23]

An Autumn's Tale then, is a lighthearted point-of-entry into a more serious discussion of complex social and historical shifts. Despite the fact that it was both critically acclaimed and commercially successful, it is the type of film often overlooked in discussions of Hong Kong cultural production. Due to the popularity of the martial arts/action films that dominate public perceptions, the melodramas, when considered at all, are marginal in discussions of Hong Kong cinema. Yet they are rich texts for both historical and cultural analysis. The second of a trilogy of diaspora stories directed by Cheung, *An Autumn's Tale* is sandwiched between her first film *The Illegal Immigrant* (1985) (a thesis project at New York University) and *Eight Taels of Gold* (1989). All three were made on small budgets, relying on help from peers associated with independent film on both sides of the Pacific and each tells the story of what it means to be "foreign" in the United States. However, it is *An Autumn's Tale* that best captures key elements of both Hong Kong and Hollywood, as well as their respective histories and cinematic traditions.

2

An Autumn's Tale as Transnational American Studies

Thanks to its connections to Hollywood (and to society and culture in the U.S. more generally), to the ever-deepening hybridization of Hong Kong and Hollywood styles, and to the flow of people and ideas across the Pacific, Hong Kong films do a particular type of cultural work, often referencing and at times both contesting and reconstructing certain "American" myths and/or histories. Migration melodramas, like many Hong Kong films, "flip the script" on Hollywood and on certain aspects of national identity, placing people who are often marginalized in mainstream films at the center of the narrative and challenging stereotypes of Chinese Americans as the model minority. Because of the way it addresses various orthodoxies within the national memory, An *Autumn's Tale* is an example of a text that is, unconsciously but effectively, performing transnational American studies. In fact, it is not the only film doing this type of cultural work. I have argued elsewhere that Hong Kong films such as *A Better Tomorrow II, Once Upon a Time in China and America, Full Moon in New York, Comrades: Almost a Love*

Story, and even Jackie Chan's Hollywood/Hong Kong hybrids *Shanghai Noon* and *Rush Hour I* and *II*, offer commentary and critique on the culture and society of the United States.[1] These films playfully reference and reconfigure identities and multiple pasts in various places and contexts. As popular culture cum transnational American studies texts, certain Hong Kong films engage multiple cultural and national myths, and in the process illustrate how myths and certain groups — from China and the U.S. — are in conversation with each other. Students and scholars looking to assess the depth of "Americanization" in Hong Kong, and the impact of migration to the U.S., will find the films rich texts for analysis.

An Autumn's Tale is typical of many Hong Kong films in its stylistic hybridity and ability to address multiple national and cultural contexts. As Esther C. M. Yau asserts, Hong Kong movies "can appear provincial yet also Hollywood-like; they have become the cultural counterpart of the 'cosmopolitan capitalist' undertakings that many Asians, especially ethnic Chinese entrepreneurs, have launched since the nineteenth century."[2] Moreover, in performing cinematic acts of revisionist history, the films make visible that which has heretofore been invisible in Hollywood. The stories told in these Hong Kong narratives of diaspora (and the personal histories of the filmmakers who move back and forth between the U.S. and Hong Kong) shed new light on old beliefs about nation and history. Additionally, the films hold up a mirror to people, places, and things "American," offering an insider/outsider perspective on life in the U.S. for the newcomer from Hong Kong.

By foregrounding the experiences of Hong Kong people who come to visit, study, and live in the U.S., *An Autumn's Tale* performs transnational American studies by engaging and critiquing, embracing and eschewing, both American and Hong Kong/Chinese notions of identity and success. The film illustrates what it feels like to encounter "America" in daily life. Cheung and Law, who, like many other Hong Kong filmmakers, actually do transit between New York and Hong Kong, offer critical commentary on Americans and their cultural myths as well as processes of Americanization. If, as Robert G. Lee has noted, "Asian American cultural producers (other than writers) have received little public visibility or critical attention," Hong Kong cultural producers — who move back and forth between Hong Kong and the U.S. thus bringing their own perspective to discussions of diaspora — have received even less.[3] Although names such as Jackie Chan and Chow Yun Fat are well known worldwide, there are many directors and screenwriters commenting on the U.S. from the vantage point of Hong Kong and it is important to include these works in discussions of contemporary U.S. (as well as Hong Kong) culture and identities. *An Autumn's Tale* is an excellent place to begin the process of considering how Hong Kong films about migration shed light on issues of identity in the United States.

In addition to expanding U.S. history and offering fresh perspectives on U.S. culture, Hong Kong films offer an alternative to the essentializing and exoticization of Chinese people and culture in Hollywood films past and present. Much has been made of Hollywood's absorption of certain Hong Kong film personalities and techniques, but a genuinely nuanced depiction of people and places from Hong Kong and/or China on Hollywood screens is still lacking. Orientalist stereotypes in films ranging from *Charlie's Angels* to Disney's *Mulan,* the recent remake of *Freaky Friday,* and *Wendy Wu: Homecoming Warrior* are typical of the way Chinese culture and identity are caricatured despite Hollywood's claims to be more sensitive to multicultural and international audiences. Hong Kong film fills a vacuum, offering stories about real people living on both sides of the Pacific. *An Autumn's Tale* is about a young Chinese woman in the U.S. who does not conform to Hollywood stereotypes yet is comfortable moving in a world where Hollywood (and American institutions generally) wields significant power.

While the central preoccupation of this study will be to examine the way *An Autumn's Tale* performs transnational American studies, other themes — particularly representations of gender and space as constructed in the film — will be explored as well. I will continue (in a more systematic fashion) the discussion of *An Autumn's Tale* and its connections to transnational American studies throughout the remainder of the book. Chapter 3 will be a brief plot summary and Chapter 4 will elucidate the film's engagement with notions of assimilation and the American dream as they relate to Chinese and Chinese American experiences in the U.S. Chapter 5 focuses on *An Autumn's Tale*'s representation of New York City, placing it in conversation with other Big Apple cinema classics. Chapter 6 concludes this look at *An Autumn's Tale* exploring the construction of gender, self-determination, and romance in diaspora.

Hong Kong films about "coming to America" help enhance our understanding of what Shelley Fisher Fishkin has called "the multiple meanings of America and American culture in all their complexity." The films casually yet cogently turn a critical eye on American Exceptionalism (the notion that there is something unique, special, or "chosen" about the American historical experience and that non-Americans can benefit by adopting various aspects of the "American way") looking beyond national boundaries, seeking an "understanding [of] how the nation is seen from vantage points beyond its borders ... a place where borders both within and outside the nation are interrogated and studied, rather than reified and reinforced."[4] If, as Henry Yu has asserted, post-national American Studies should "strive to place nation formation within transnational contexts of racial and cultural differentiation," *An Autumn's Tale* does just that even as it entertains and delivers a happy ending (Still 2.1).[5]

Still 2.1   *An Autumn's Tale*: Jenny (Cherie Chung) and Figgy (Chow Yun Fat) stroll along the beach. Both are subject to processes of "Americanization" albeit in different ways.

3

Plot Summary of
An Autumn's Tale

An Autumn's Tale begins with the arrival of Jenny (Cherie Chung) in New York City where she will join her boyfriend, Vincent (Danny Chan) and attend graduate school. Retired sailor and n'er-do-well, Samuel Pang (Chow Yun Fat) — also nicknamed "Boathead," "Figurehead," or "Figgy" — is a distant "cousin" of Jenny's who has agreed to meet her at the airport. Figgy and his friends arrive late to collect Jenny (they have been gambling in Atlantic City) but Figgy helps her settle into a run-down Chinatown apartment where he is the building manager. While Figgy constantly reminds Jenny that "women are chable" (a play on the Cantonese phrase for tea bowl as well as a "Chinglish" pronunciation of the word "trouble"), he does offer her support in a number of ways as she adjusts to New York City. While she is still getting her bearings, she learns that Vincent (the boyfriend she has followed to America) has another girlfriend and that he has decided to move to Boston. When Jenny expresses her anger at Vincent's duplicity, he tells her not to be upset because, after all, "Over here [in the U.S.] girls are liberal-minded."

Jenny's culture shock turns to depression and Figgy tries to comfort her (albeit without much success). One early autumn evening, Jenny is so despondent she doesn't notice a gas leak in her dilapidated kitchen. Exhausted and nearly overcome by fumes leaking from her stove, Jenny's life is in danger. Figgy smells the fumes and he rushes to save her. In an attempt to keep the apartment from burning, firefighters break windows and damage Jenny's already inhospitable (and still unfamiliar) home. Figgy, now more determined than ever to see Jenny heal and regain confidence, helps her remodel the apartment and settle into her life as a student at New York University. As the autumn progresses, Jenny gradually becomes more comfortable at school and she secures a part-time job working for a single Chinese American mother (Mrs. Sherwood) babysitting her daughter Anna. The Sherwoods live in an affluent suburb in Long Island. In the meantime, although Figgy has helped Jenny adjust, his own position in the city is somewhat precarious. His days are spent with friends who, like himself, are waiting tables and doing other odd jobs. They spend their nights hustling and picking fights with others who live on the margins of the city.

Despite differences in class backgrounds, Jenny and Figgy fall in love although neither is able to express their true feelings. When Mrs. Sherwood's boyfriend (who has also hired Jenny as a waitress in his Chinese restaurant) tries to sexually harass her, Figgy beats him up, and helps Jenny get back on her feet. As they spend more time together, the two discuss their dreams and ambitions for the future. Jenny, who is by now quite confident in her independence, declares that she wants to see the world. Figgy retorts that he's had enough of travel. His dream is to open a restaurant by the sea. The two become even closer and when Figgy decides to host a party on his 24th birthday, he encourages Jenny to invite some of her school friends. Jenny's old boyfriend Vincent shows up unexpectedly and wants to reconcile with her. Feeling intimidated by Vincent's return, Figgy leaves the party and joins his gambling buddies for a night of drinking and fighting. When the party ends and there is still no sign of Figgy, Jenny decides to wait up for him. She cleans his room while she waits and in the process she realizes that it is his birthday, and that he has been working to become more assimilated to the United States and more like the wealthy men he sees surrounding Jenny (Vincent and Mrs. Sherwood's boyfriend). Jenny sees that Figgy is "becoming an American" in order to win her love and approval. When there is still no sign of Figgy the next morning, Jenny goes for a walk to ease her mind. In a nearby park she is surprised to meet Mrs. Sherwood and Anna. They want her to move to the house on Long Island with them. Jenny — who by now has given up hope that she and Figgy will be together — agrees to do so.

In the meantime, Figgy returns home and sees that Jenny has tidied his room and left him a birthday gift. Hoping that he now has a chance for a more permanent relationship with her, he runs to an antique dealer and trades his car for an expensive watchband he knows Jenny likes. Sans car, Figgy dashes through the streets of lower Manhattan, racing back to the apartment to present his gift to Jenny. When he returns, he finds Jenny loading her belongings into Vincent's car. (Although she and Vincent have not reconciled, Jenny accepts his offer of a ride to the Sherwoods'.) Figgy assumes that Jenny and Vincent have been reunited and his misreading of the situation keeps him from expressing his love for Jenny. In a scene that invokes O. Henry's famous short story, "The Gift of the Magi," the two exchange goodbye gifts. The audience realizes that Jenny has given Figgy her antique watch for which he has purchased a watchband. Despite an attempt to run after Vincent's car, Figgy is left behind in Chinatown while Jenny moves to the suburbs of Long Island. However, a year later, as the result of a chance encounter, the two friends meet again along the Atlantic waterfront where they had strolled together months before. Jenny sees that Figgy — now the thoroughly Americanized Samuel Pang

— has realized his dream of owning a seaside restaurant, fittingly titled "Sam Pan." After a dramatic pause, Figgy flashes a charming smile and invites Jenny to enjoy a table for two.

4

An Autumn's Tale, Assimilation, and the American Dream

Although there are many powerful myths and ideologies that circulate in U.S. society, among the most powerful is the notion of the American dream. While there is no one specific definition of the dream, Americans generally understand the meaning to be that if one works hard, opportunities for success are plentiful in the United States. As Jennifer L. Hochschild has noted in her work on the ideology of the American dream, the dream is the "faith that an individual can attain success and virtue through strenuous efforts."[1] The connection between the newly arrived immigrant and the American dream in literature is present in well-known texts by diverse authors such as Anzia Yezierska, Jane Addams, Gus Lee, Amy Tan, Younghill Kang, and Carlos Bulosan. On the big screen, the quest for (and often failure to fulfill) the American dream is among Hollywood's most favored plotlines. Stories of immigrants who come to the U.S. (and often New York City) to pursue happiness and success include iconic films such as *The Godfather, Avalon, Coming to America, Far and Away,* and *Titanic.*

The popularity of American dream narratives spills beyond the geographic borders of the United States. Many people from various countries travel to and from "America" in virtual (via popular culture) and real time, in the process re-fashioning and claiming the dream as their own. In the case of Hong Kong — dubbed by Milton Friedman as the ultimate free market economy — it is not surprising that much of the rhetoric of aspiration within civil society parallels that which circulates in the U.S. Narratives of upward mobility and economic success circulate freely in the media, as if to prove that "making it" in Hong Kong is well within reach regardless of who is in charge — Britain before 1997, Beijing after. In the American Studies courses I have taught at the University of Hong Kong, I notice that students warm to the notion of the dream. They believe that Hong Kong offers opportunities for success if they are willing to work hard enough, and they see the notion as universal rather than American.

In the climate of uncertainty that has marked much of Hong Kong's past, as well as its present, self-reliance offers some refuge. For students at least, and arguably for many in Hong Kong who have access to American ideology via travel, exchange, dual citizenship, or popular culture, the rhetoric of the dream offers hope and a possible way forward. Despite (or perhaps because of) colonialism before 1997, and the still evolving paternalism of Beijing in the present, Hong Kong people generally embrace individual narratives of self-improvement over critiques of structural or institutional inadequacy. Hong Kong migration films both affirm and critique the embrace. Canny in their knowledge of various power dynamics in the postcolonial/global-imperial rush for diverse types of capital among governments, corporations, and individuals, films like *An Autumn's Tale* enter the conversation about aspiration and migration in a moment of "flexible citizenship."[2] Critiquing not only the American dream but American multiculturalism and the "comforting narratives of liberal inclusion" that mask U.S.

imperialism at home and abroad (something that scholars such as Victor Bascara and others in Asian American and Postcolonial Studies are doing more intentionally), migration melodramas like *An Autumn's Tale* manage to simultaneously affirm and lampoon the "self-made man" mentality on both sides of the Pacific.[3]

As Hong Kong films interrogate various "American" cultural orthodoxies, they also manage to subtly explore repressed historical connections between the U.S. and Hong Kong/China. Pushing the discussion of race and ethnicity in the U.S. beyond the Black and White binary, Hong Kong films often simultaneously claim and contest the American dream for the post-1965 Hong Kong Chinese "astronaut." In the process, they offer a view of multiculturalism that is more than a cliché. As Kwai-Cheung Lo writes, since "the Asian role is not fixated in the dominant racial discourse, Hong Kong film people can take the opportunity to go between one culture and another and increase their agency in remaking the transnational codification of their identity."[4] In the case of *An Autumn's Tale,* the transnational codification of self is in process for the characters on screen as well as for many of those involved in the film's production. This is significant because, as historian Ronald Takaki reminds us, the story of multicultural America requires looking at a variety of sources (and I would add "non-American" sources in the case of Hong Kong films like *An Autumn's Tale*) in order to understand what has been left out of previous accounts of the nation and its past.

By "telling and retelling" what happened, Takaki writes, "the people of multicultural America brush against the grain of the master narrative of American history, the ethnocentric story told from the perspective of the English colonists and their descendants. They break a silence imposed on them."[5] Hong Kong films such as *An Autumn's Tale*, *Once Upon a Time in China and America,* and Hollywood/Hong Kong hybrid *Shanghai Noon* remind audiences of Asian points of entry into a larger story of the movement of

Chinese people to America, gently nudging European immigration narratives away from center stage by adding to an emerging body of stories (in literature and society at large) about those who came to the U.S. from Asia. Audiences are reminded that people flowed from the west to the east as well as from east to west in the process of nation building. As we watch Jenny and Figgy become "new Americans" in *An Autumn's Tale,* we also see the U.S. as a site of cross/multicultural contact. However, the claim on multiculturalism is not, to use Robert G. Lee's words, "a premature celebration of a multicultural utopia." As Lee and other scholars in Asian American studies have argued, "multiculturalism serves the state in its management of difference, obscuring contradictions of contemporary globalization and the savage inequalities that it has generated." Hong Kong films offer critical commentary on multiculturalism while still seeking to recoup it as an important (albeit troubled) concept.[6]

Like Takaki, Gary Okihiro asserts that perspectives from Asia are key to understanding American history in a more comprehensive light. He suggests that we think more consciously about "how Asians helped to redefine the meaning of American identity, to expand it beyond the narrower idea of only white and black, and to move it beyond the confines of the American state and the prescribed behaviors of loyalty and patriotism."[7] Clearly, while films — even those based on "true" stories — take tremendous leeway with the "facts" and a film like *An Autumn's Tale* makes no claim to be historical, it is a story about an actual historical phenomenon — the migration of large numbers of upwardly mobile Hong Kong people to the U.S. in the late 20th century. Okihiro writes that "new Americans," mostly Latinos and Asians, established communities in the U.S. and the 1980s was a particularly important time of change.

This demographic shift can be measured in terms of population growth and increased minority group influence in many corners of

U.S. society. From 1980 to 1990, while the White population grew by 4.3 percent nationally, Asian Americans increased by 13 percent, Latinos by 49.8 percent and Asians by 93.9 percent."[8] During the 1980s, several significant events marked the rising influence of Chinese Americans within the United States. Lily Lee Chen was elected Mayor of Monterey Park, California (the first Chinese American woman to hold a mayoral post in the U.S.). Also during this period many U.S. cities became the beneficiaries of new arrivals (and capital) from Greater China, particularly Hong Kong. Neighborhoods in cities as geographically distant as Oakland, California and New York's Chinatown were able to revitalize during the 1980s as a result.[9] *An Autumn's Tale* is a Hong Kong cinematic accompaniment to Asian American/ethnic history scholarship documenting demographic shifts (in both the 19th and the 20th centuries), and telling the story of how change took place at the micro level. Jenny and Figgy are two quasi-fictional characters but their stories symbolize those of thousands of Hong Kong people who came to the United States at the end of the 20th century.

In discussing the demographics of migration from the Hong Kong side, Chu Yingchi asserts that because a real departure from Hong Kong was not an option available to most of its residents, after the mid-1980s "it became almost a fashion for local filmmakers to create some sort of narrative connection with overseas, offering a fantasy for local spectators to vicariously experience life in the West."[10] Hong Kong films share common ground with the Asian American cultural texts that Lisa Lowe discusses in her work in that they "offer other modes for imagining and narrating immigrant subjectivity and community — emerging out of conditions of decolonization, displacement, and disidentification — and refuse assimilation into dominant narratives of integration, development and identification."[11] The characters in *An Autumn's Tale* embrace the American dream to a certain extent but also stand apart from it, as will be discussed in more detail hereafter.

Although multiple stories linked to European immigration have been represented on Hollywood's screens for decades, Asian immigration, particularly in the post-1965 era has, with a few exceptions, been sidelined in Hollywood. A rich documentary film tradition revealing and/or engaging with previously invisible histories in such works as Tsui Hark's *Spikes and Spindles*, Felicia Lowe's *Carved in Silence*, or Renee Tajima Peña's *My America: or Honk if You Love Buddha*, fills this void to a certain extent, but commercially successful films about Asian immigration to the U.S. (with the exception of *The Joy Luck Club* and *Heaven and Earth*) are still few in number. Hollywood continues to caricature or exoticize late-20th century immigrants from Asia, even in films such as the critically acclaimed 2005 Oscar winner, *Crash*. Yet as Lisa Lowe reminds us, "Understanding Asian immigration to the United States is fundamental to understanding the racialized foundations of both the emergence of the United States as a nation and the development of American capitalism."[12] While it is not a political film, *An Autumn's Tale* subtly points to certain links between consumer economies in Asia and the U.S., in the process gently prodding audiences to think about attitudes toward and the treatment of Hong Kong people in the U.S. at the end of the 20th century.

Not only does *An Autumn's Tale* open up a space for a reconsideration of the past, it sheds light on the connections between Hong Kong and America that couple the national to the individual and intimate. Jenny is a newcomer to the U.S. but she comes from a community (and a class background) where people are comfortable transiting back and forth across the Pacific Ocean. She arrives in New York knowing that her "distant cousin," Figgy, will be waiting to meet her. She speaks fluent English and understands various cultural references that circulate in the U.S. because she is familiar with American popular culture through her Hong Kong upbringing. The "American" nation can be accessed, and the "American" dream claimed from many places beyond the geographical boundaries of the U.S. Gina Marchetti has written about the various ways American popular culture becomes part of Hong Kong's urban culture. She notes that Hong Kong films are constantly defining, contesting, making and un-making images of "America." [13] As a result of her identity as a Hong Kong person, Jenny "knows" the U.S. in many respects even before she has set foot there.

Figgy, like Jenny, strikes a transnational pose as he engages and interrogates mythic notions of immigrant success and the American dream. At various points in the film we see him quoting famous Americans (such as George Washington). Figgy helps Jenny become "Americanized" without compromising (too much) of her Chinese-ness. Early on in the film, Figgy tells Jenny to work hard and refuse to let people look down on her. He reminds her of George Washington's declaration that, "a good start is half way to success." When Jenny queries him as to whether or not Washington really did say such a thing, Figgy replies, "If not Washington then it must be Confucius. Either one!"

In his flippant attitude about notions of achievement in China and in the United States, Figgy playfully mixes various ideologies, conflating Confucianism and Americanism as celebrated through acquisition of means and virtue. Aspiration is, for Figgy and his friends, coded as both (or neither) American and Chinese. Playfully mocking two beloved national leaders and icons, Figgy quips that Confucian and American notions of success are quite similar. In the end, it is up to the individual to find his or her own way regardless of national myths or cultural expectations. Although Figgy does struggle at various points in the film to survive financially, he maintains a casual attitude about earning and spending. He is carefree about winning and losing money, cars, and other material possessions. Two of his favorite phrases are "No money no worries," and "Nothing matters as long as I'm happy."

In some places during *An Autumn's Tale* we are reminded that Figgy's posturing is, indeed, masking his own class anxieties, but up until the conclusion of the film when he is transformed into the self-made man who runs his own restaurant by the sea, he serves as a foil for those who plunge headlong into accumulating without considering needs or deeper meanings. The fact that Figgy ends up as an exemplar of the dream is a final bit of irony in *An Autumn's Tale.*

Notions of the American dream are invoked at another key point near the end of the film when Jenny discovers a list of goals Figgy has written and posted on the mirror in his bedroom. It is here that Jenny (and the audience) comes to understand the power of the ideology of the dream for Figgy (and perhaps for many new immigrants). It appears that despite his protests to Jenny and his friends that he does not need money to be happy, his encounters with upwardly mobile Americans including Jenny's boyfriend Vincent, as well her boss (who owns an upscale Chinese restaurant), have affected him quite deeply. Jenny realizes that Figgy has expended significant effort as he has worked to become more financially successful as well as more fully assimilated to the U.S. It is clear that he is hoping to become a more attractive suitor for Jenny and he ties the two desires — economic success and love — together in his credo (Still 4.1) which reads:

> Diligence is the key to success
> Get the green card then the gold card
> Wear shoes, wear socks
> Speak grammatical English
> If you want it, go for it!

As Figgy appropriates American ideology and phrases for his own purposes, he is both playful and knowing. He realizes that in order to make money ("Get the gold card") he will first have to become a citizen with a green card. The use of colloquial American phrases

Still 4.1 *An Autumn's Tale*: Figgy reviews his plan
for economic and romantic success

such as "go for it!" also reveal an attempt at trying on American
identity through language. Throughout the film, Figgy struggles to
move back and forth between his "Chinese" and "American" selves
but it is apparent that he believes the self-improvement project
will enhance his efforts to assimilate into American, particularly
New York, society.

Just as Hong Kong films offer insights into processes of
assimilation and the construction of national identity in the U.S.,
they reflect on many of the same issues in terms of Hong Kong
identity. Characterizing Hong Kong as a "quasi-nation" because of
its colonial past and its status as a Special Administrative Region
of the PRC, Yingchi Chu acknowledges the significance of film and
popular culture in helping to shape Hong Kong's sense of self.[14]
Chu argues that Hong Kong film in the 1980s and 1990s became a
"forum for the construction, exploration and questioning of Hong
Kong's sense of nationhood."[15] In subtle ways, throughout the film,
An Autumn's Tale bears witness to Hong Kong's quasi-nationality
through its citizens who are mobile and comfortable in New York,
yet strongly identified with the home they left behind. It is because
of her Hong Kong contacts in New York's Chinatown that Jenny

survives in the city, finds various jobs, and becomes more comfortable on her own in Manhattan. On the other hand, Figgy and his friends resist learning English, and they frequent game halls reminiscent of those they knew in Hong Kong. Jenny and Figgy take different paths to assimilation but both rely upon their Hong Kong pasts as a basis for forging new identities in the United States. *An Autumn's Tale* fleshes out various experiences from within the Chinese diaspora and it examines the specific impact of the "brain drain" as it reveals varying strands of Hong Kong quasi-national identities.

Many Hong Kong films produced at the end of the 20th century (besides *An Autumn's Tale*) addressed the ripple effects of out migration, focusing on the experiences of people leaving Hong Kong because of the uncertainty of their fates in the lead-up to 1997. While more than 850,000 Hong Kongers arrived in the U.S. between 1965 and 1990, hundreds of thousands chose other destinations.[16] As they spread across the world, many still identified strongly with both Hong Kong (quasi-nationality?) and a diffuse Chinese-ness (albeit expressed differently according to individual circumstance). As such, *An Autumn's Tale* speaks to diasporic audiences comprised of many individuals who are managing various levels of connection to both new homes in the U.S. and old homes in Asia. Jenny is a particularly compelling cinematic prototype. Not only does she serve as a model of a young woman who manages to achieve her American dream, she succeeds in the U.S. without turning her back on Hong Kong. Instead, she crafts a new identity that represents the possibility of holding on to Hong Kong and facilitating pan-Chinese bonding even as she becomes more Americanized. One subtle example of this occurs as Jenny and Figgy finish their restoration work on her Chinatown apartment. Jenny lovingly places three flags- one from the U.S., one from the PRC, and one from Taiwan — into a vase, prominently displayed in her freshly repainted living room (Still 4.2).

Still 4.2 *An Autumn's Tale*: Jenny displays flags from the U.S., Taiwan, and the PRC in her newly renovated Chinatown apartment.

In fact, the "romance" in the film invoked by the Chinese title (literally "An Autumn's Fairy Tale") is not just the spark that ignites between Jenny and Figgy. Another type of romance is an idealistic, pre-Tiananmen optimism about upward mobility, multicultural adjustment, and Chinese-ness among various sub-ethnic groups in New York City. Jenny's eagerness to display three "national" flags side by side (as already noted) is one example of such a stance but there are others. Near the end of the film Figgy declares with pride that all Chinese men are experienced fighters. (Ironically, the actual fighting scenes in the film do not confirm this assertion.) The two gang fights that take place in *An Autumn's Tale* seem comic rather than a heroic demonstration of prowess. As such, the Chow we have come to know on global screens is not present in *An Autumn's Tale*. Still, it is clear that Figgy prizes particular "Chinese" ways of fighting and he sees this as a source of pan-Chinese male bonding. (Of course this reinforces certain Hollywood stereotypes about which more will be said in the final chapter.) In its assertion that "we Chinese" have much in common, the film manifests an almost quaint optimism that sets it apart from other darkly realistic post-

1989 migration films such as Clara Law's *Farewell China* and Evans Chan's *Crossings.*

Hong Kong migration films, then, are not just examples of transnational American studies in action. To a certain extent, they are also important artifacts of cultural history. Despite the fact that they are, for the most part, stories of fictional folk in a new place, they are something more. Taken as a body of work on the subject of the changes taking place for a generation of "astronauts," the Hong Kong migration melodramas of Cheung and Law, Evans Chan, Stanley Kwan, Ann Hui, Alex Law, and Eddie Fong, chronicle an eventful period — the 1980s and 1990s — and tell a range of stories of people who left Hong Kong for new lives elsewhere. The final destination may have been the United States, the United Kingdom, Australia, Canada, New Zealand, Europe, or somewhere in between, but all who left packed their connection to Hong Kong and its unique culture and history in their travel bags.[17] However, *An Autumn's Tale*'s idealistic tone reflects another link to history in that it was released two years before tanks rolled into Beijing. From the vantage point of the present, the film's optimism marks its connections to a very different time and place.

"Others" in *An Autumn's Tale*

In addition to broadening the discussion of traditional immigrant narratives beyond European American experiences, *An Autumn's Tale* also opens up a space for the conceptualization of a more complex and multicultural past, as well as capturing the mood of many New Yorkers living through a period of economic uncertainty and the 1980s culture wars. Yet the film also reinforces certain stereotypes as it contests others. In this respect, the film shares common ground with John Woo's *A Better Tomorrow II* (1987) and Jackie Chan's *Rumble in the Bronx* (1995). All of these films, to a certain extent, portray the U.S. as a wasteland of racism and violence. Ironically, then, at the same time *An Autumn's Tale* succeeds as a narrative of multicultural America that places Chinese and Chinese American experiences as a central focus, the portrayal of other ethnic groups is quite wooden. Additionally, questions of race and ethnicity are engaged unevenly in the film.

The juxtaposition of a range of nuanced characterizations of Chinese with more stereotypical portrayals of other groups is a bit jarring. Most problematic are the portrayals of non-White, non-Chinese groups, particularly Blacks and Latinos. The film misses an opportunity to explore the links between the individual and collective struggles of various minority groups to assimilate into the U.S. mainstream. As a result, *An Autumn's Tale*'s treatment of race and ethnicity is limited. Black and Latino characters in the film are presented as violent and threatening to outsiders who keep New York City from being safe and free. Representatives of the two non-Asian minority groups featured in the film represent the limits of the American dream and are associated with deviance and danger. This pattern is established early in the film. When Figgy and his friends meet Jenny at the airport they encounter a Black security guard who informs them they cannot park near the terminal entrance. They claim they do not understand English — in fact they pretend to be Japanese in a playful referent to the stereotype that Americans think "all Asians look alike" — in order to escape from the security guard's wrath. The guard appears weak and incompetent (Still 4.3). In the next scene, as Figgy and his friends chauffeur Jenny home from the airport, they are accosted by a group of Puerto Rican Americans (Figgy identifies them as Mexican Americans) shouting obscenities and trying to run Figgy and his friends off the road. Once they arrive in Manhattan, they are hassled by a Black man who wants money to clean the windshield he has covered in soapsuds. Later in the film, as Jenny and Figgy walk through the streets of the city, they often encounter Black men who are drunk, angry, or vagrants.

Still 4.3 *An Autumn's Tale*: Figgy and his friends take advantage of an airport security guard. Depictions of Blacks and Latinos in *An Autumn's Tale* often reinforce rather than challenge racist stereotypes.

For those who have actually lived or spent a significant amount of time in various Manhattan neighborhoods (the author lived in New York City for over six years in the late 1980s and early 1990s), the characterizations seem extreme. One might argue that *An Autumn's Tale* reproduces ethnic stereotypes in order to explore racism against newly arrived Chinese in New York City, but White racism remains unexamined. Director Mabel Cheung Yuen-ting believes that the film accurately reflects the anxieties internalized by recent arrivals from Hong Kong and other parts of Asia. From the critical standpoint of the 21st century, however, the images remain problematic.[18] The portrayals are particularly troubling because Asian Americans have been stereotyped as the model minority; a group supposedly succeeding where African Americans and Latinos have not. While there is more evidence to contradict than to support this assertion, it continues to thrive in many corners of American society. As such, a Hong Kong film that reproduces negative images of certain minority groups can easily (albeit likely unconsciously) foment misunderstanding. Capitalizing on cross-minority group tensions rather than addressing the complex factors facilitating or restricting racial equality and economic success in the contemporary United States, the film reinforces traditional thinking.[19]

For the most part, White EuroAmerican characters are seen as insignificant in the film. This is an interesting and important departure from other immigrant films where tensions between Whites and minority groups often figure prominently in the narrative. Jenny is clearly surrounded by White classmates at New York University who first ignore and later befriend her, but they don't speak in the film. One White character is a surly police officer who tries to keep Figgy from re-selling Broadway tickets he is unable to use and another is one of Mrs. Sherwood's many boyfriends. They both seem indifferent and unwilling to acknowledge Jenny and Figgy. The one White person in the film who does engage with the two leads is an elderly antique store dealer and he is a very minor character in the film. One way to read this absence is that the film deliberately excludes the White majority because it is so often the subject of Hollywood's narrative focus and this is a film about the Chinese diaspora in New York City. However, another interpretation is that whiteness is such a hegemonic presence; it is taken for granted, even if it is not seen in the film. It is also possible that the negative portrayals of Blacks and Latinos, and the narrative insignificance of Whites, reflect Cheung and Law's own newcomer status in the U.S. at the time the film was made. As such, their "real life" encounters with other non-Chinese groups were limited, or they occurred at a very surface level.

As noted above, Cheung and Law defend the depiction of various ethnic groups in the film and they caution against overanalyzing the depiction of ethnic tension in *An Autumn's Tale*. They say that their intent in making the film was to keep it as honest and as real as possible, while still preserving a certain idealism in terms of the relationship that develops between Jenny and Figgy. They see their depictions of non-Chinese in the film as reflective of reality for many people living in Chinatown. The misnaming of Puerto Rican Americans and Mexican Americans, or the expressions of curiosity about and/or fear of Blacks on midtown Manhattan streets is typical behavior for those who prefer the comfort and homogeneity of Chinatown to more ethnically diverse parts of the city.

According to Cheung and Law, many Chinese immigrants who come to New York simply do not have much contact with those who do not share a similar ethnic background. The real person on whom the character of Figgy was based was, in fact, quite uncomfortable when he was outside of his Chinatown comfort zone. Cheung and Law note that when he and his friends actually ventured out, they did indeed view others as "foreigners" and they often mislabeled or misjudged those who were not Chinese due to their own insularity. It is this narrow view that Cheung and Law were keen to interrogate and encourage their audience to move beyond.[20]

The film also makes a subtle statement about differences between various sub-ethnic groups of people of Chinese descent in the U.S. Although it is difficult to discern from the film itself, Cheung reminds her audience to keep in mind that while Figgy spent time in Hong Kong prior to going to the United States, he was, originally, from the Chinese mainland. He lived through the Cultural Revolution, where he had much less exposure to western ideas and influences than Jenny, who was born and raised in Hong Kong. She identifies with aspects of British as well as Chinese culture. For Jenny (like Cheung herself), most of her schooling was conducted in English. As such, she is comfortable in a more westernized urban setting which, in many respects, has more in common with New York than it does with cities in the PRC. Not all members of the Chinese diaspora are on equal footing when they arrive in the "land of the free." *An Autumn's Tale* serves as a subtle reminder of the individual differences that are obscured by generalizations about Hong Kong's quasi-national identity. The film also provides an opportunity to interrogate racism — subtle or blatant — in the United States, in Hong Kong, or elsewhere.

Happy Endings and the American Dream

At the conclusion of *An Autumn's Tale,* the ideal of the American dream is invoked one last time as we see Jenny and Figgy as confidently assimilated Americans. In the final scene, as Jenny strolls along the beach chatting with Anna, we learn that one year has passed since she left Chinatown to move in with Anna and her mother on Long Island. Jenny looks fashionable and confident (Still 4.4). Hair now styled and straightened, shawl draped casually across her shoulder, she looks very much at home. Jenny tells Anna about her friend Figgy, who wanted to own a seaside restaurant nearby. Anna points to a restaurant in the distance named "Sam

Still 4.4 *An Autumn's Tale*: Near the conclusion of the film, a confident and Americanized Jenny strolls along the beach with her babysitting charge, Anna.

Pan" and Jenny realizes that indeed, Figgy has fulfilled his dream. As she nears the entrance to the restaurant, she sees her old friend and he greets her with a smile. Dressed stylishly in a dark suit, with a red power tie (it is the 1980s after all), his flyaway hair has been cut, oiled, and slicked back, making him look more urbane. He has shed all traces of his shady past. Owning his own business means that he no longer needs gambling to "balance his mind." Figgy, now the thoroughly Americanized Samuel Pang, welcomes Jenny to his restaurant and asks her if she'd like a table for two. With the sun setting over his shoulder and the sound of waves gently rolling onto the beach, the fairy-tale reading of the film's conclusion suggests that the couple will live happily ever after as class, gender, and ethnic differences are swept away with the tide (Still 4.5).

Still 4.5   *An Autumn's Tale*: Jenny and Figgy are reunited in the fairy-tail conclusion of the film. Figgy now owns his own restaurant by the sea.

Writing about the film's conclusion, Lisa Odham Stokes and Michael Hoover envision "smooth sailing in America for this acclimated couple in the days ahead," although each models a different path to success and acceptance in America. "Figgy's attitude towards life, which involves his remaining in a close-knit community of men like himself, reflects one way of dealing with the émigré predicament," Odham Stokes and Hoover assert. Figgy sticks close to his buddies. Jenny, on the other hand, is able to rely on a broad network of friends thanks to her privileged class background and facility with English.[21]

Julian Stringer proffers a different interpretation of *An Autumn's Tale*'s ending. He sees Jenny and Figgy's different class backgrounds as shaping the "formation of their Asian American identities." As such, Figgy's future seems more uncertain than Jenny's. This is because he is "left to mingle and fight with the neighborhood Chinese gangs ... Despite his aspiration to 'get the green card, then the gold card,' Sam Pan has no means to move out of Chinatown ..." For Stringer, Figgy's experiences "could form the basis of a new ethnic pride and consciousness, or they could lead to his stigmatization via the terms of the sojourner mentality."[22] Stringer clearly has little use for the fairy-tale-like coda at the end of the film. He predicts that Jenny will, eventually, "hook up once more with the economically mobile Vincent." The only conclusion to be drawn is that "Sam Pan is left to face a bleak future alone in Chinatown." Dismissing the beach scene at the end of *An Autumn's Tale* as literally imaginary, Stringer quips, "A final scene reunites Jennifer and Sam Pan, but the meeting is revealed as nothing more than a fantasy projection (hers? his?)."[23]

Stringer also points out that despite the glitz of the city portrayed on screen in this diaspora film, New York is less than romantic for people like Figgy. He notes, "As Sam Pan's experiences in *An Autumn's Tale* testify, the reality is that overseas Chinese more often than not end up trapped and exploited within economically depressed ghettos."[24] As Kwai-Cheung Lo reminds us, although these films "could be considered transnational in their inclinations, these works still see the foreign other as a differentiating entity from which a distinct Hong Kong or Chinese identity is constituted."[25] Figgy may help Jenny to feel more at home in New York City, but he maintains a very "Hong Kong" existence himself. Stringer notes that it is gambling which provides Figgy both solace and relief, and a connection to his Hong Kong past. As a locale that was much invoked in 1980s Hong Kong films (particularly those starring Chow such as *God of Gamblers* and *God of Gamblers Returns*), it is no accident that Cheung uses the gambling den as Figgy's refuge. Stringer argues that the use of gambling as metaphor raises several issues "about the restructuring of economic relations between Hong Kong and New York, about the hopes and disappointments that accompany overseas migration, and about how gambling in Chinatown can itself provide the cause of nothing but trouble and strife."[26]

In fact, Stringer's read on Figgy's fate and the film's conclusion may not be far off the mark. The person who served as the real-life model for the character of Figgy did not open a restaurant facing the ocean. Although he was involved in helping with set construction during the time the crew was filming in New York, he ended up in prison for several years. Cheung notes that precisely because the real Figgy lived such a tragic life, she and Law decided to modify the narrative, letting romance rather than reality modify and ultimately supersede actual events. In an interview with Cheung and Law, we discussed their decision to "give our friend [Figgy] a restaurant by the sea" in the film because in reality, he was not so lucky:

> **Cheung:** Yes, in real life, it was so sad. He went to prison and he was betrayed. But in the film, as a director, I could give him a restaurant ... I am the creator of this film so I insisted. At that time there was a difference of opinion about the ending. My producers said to me you can end with the scene where they parted and Chow Yun Fat is standing underneath the bridge looking at the watch. But I felt like I wanted to give a restaurant to my friend.

Law: But at the time we made the film, he was still living there [in New York]. Whatever else happened to him happened after we were finished shooting. It's a sad story. But he was there, and he helped us build the Sam Pan Restaurant by the waterfront. And what's funny is that when I went there, I looked at the set and I said to myself, hey, there's a spelling mistake here. It doesn't say Sam Pan, it says Sam Man. And it was him, he'd made the sign ... But I thought I shouldn't change it. After all, it's him ... he was the kind of guy who would spell his name wrong. If you look at the film again you'll see that it says Sam Man not Sam Pan.[27] (Still 4.6)

Still 4.6 *An Autumn's Tale*: Director Mabel Cheung Yuen-ting and scriptwriter Alex Law decide against correcting the spelling error in the title of the Sam Pan Restaurant.

So, in spite of the fact that "real" Figgy's life in New York (post-Hong Kong) was no fairy tale, the film tells a different story. *An Autumn's Tale* leaves its audience with the impression that class differences do not matter or can be easily overcome, and that young, single women can "make it" in New York with just a little help and support.

As mentioned earlier, the film's hopeful view of Chinese assimilation and achievement in the U.S. stands in marked contrast to other Hong Kong migration narratives set in New York City such as Clara Law's *Farewell China* and Evans Chan's *Crossings*. In these films, the pathos of marginalization, misunderstanding, and discrimination are central preoccupations. Endings are marked by loss, separation, feelings of ennui, or even death. (Although the concluding scenes of Peter Chan's *Comrades: Almost a Love Story* and Stanley Kwan's *Full Moon in New York* are more upbeat than *Farewell China* and *Crossings*, compared to the "happily ever after" tone of *An Autumn's Tale*, the other migration stories appear downright dour.) While it engages many of the same themes and probes many of the issues engaged in other Hong Kong migration melodramas, *An Autumn's Tale* strikes a hopeful (and typically American) chord about the possibilities of adjustment to U.S. society. Jenny and Figgy both end up as assimilated American citizens, living productive lives and realizing their individual dreams. *An Autumn's Tale* leaves the audience with little doubt that newcomers can find a place where they feel at home, despite the very real difficulties they must endure.

Many of those involved in making *An Autumn's Tale* wanted the ending to take place one scene earlier, where Jenny and Vincent speed away in Vincent's convertible, and, unbeknownst to Jenny, Figgy chases along behind. Cheung opted for the fairy-tale ending on the beach, holding out hope to the children of the Hong Kong (and pan-Chinese) diaspora that a "happily ever after" really is possible. Cheung is well aware that in reality there has always been (and still is) discrimination against Chinese and Chinese Americans living in the U.S. Despite relaxation of immigrant quotas, legislative gains, increases in the native and foreign-born populations of individuals of Chinese as well as of Asian descent within the United States, and a belief in the importance of multiculturalism as a metaphor to replace or at least accompany the antiquated notion of the melting pot, those who are often labeled as members of the "model minority" do not have an easy time of it in the U.S. As Lisa Lowe laments, "A national memory haunts the conception of the Asian American," and the memory continues to persist "beyond the repeal of actual laws prohibiting Asians from citizenship and sustained by the wars in Asia, in which the Asian is always seen as an immigrant, as the 'foreigner-within,' even when born in the United States and the descendant of generations born here before."[28] As Gina Marchetti asserts, "The promise of prosperity in Hong Kong and New York is undercut by the harsh conditions for immigrants in both places."[29] Yet despite painful historical realities and ongoing prejudice, the film stands firmly on the side of hope that things can improve and that people evolve. *An Autumn's Tale* recreates immigrant narratives in a hopeful light, telling the story of success as well as suffering and displacement.

A more complex reading of *An Autumn's Tale*'s conclusion tempers idealism with realism. Despite the hope and happy ending, there are some interesting omissions and tensions present in the film. A critical eye cannot ignore the narrative gap between the penultimate and final scenes. The audience is not offered any clue as to how Figgy is actually able to achieve his American dream of owning a restaurant by the sea. We see Jenny travel along on her path to assimilation but Figgy "arrives" without much explanation along the way. It seems that Cheung can tell her own story — the story of a middle-class woman from Hong Kong "making it" in the U.S. — more easily than she can tell Figgy's story. Is it, perhaps, more difficult to craft a credible discussion of the path to achievement and assimilation for a working-class Chinese man in New York City? Perhaps the ending itself indicates a certain ambivalence about assimilation, despite the "happily ever after" tone of the last scene. Except for the "imaginary" finale where Figgy is dressed like a Wall Street executive, we never actually see Figgy compromise his Chinese-ness. The same cannot be said for other characters in *An Autumn's Tale*. Jenny and Mrs. Sherwood (the two most truly assimilated characters in the film) have had to transform themselves (in terms of looks, attitudes, and geographic space. They both "leave" Chinatown for the suburbs) in order to become "real" Americans. Because we are not witness to Figgy's transformation, we are subtly encouraged to accept (without proof) another fantasy (and a significant counter to the beloved dream and immigrant mythology). That fantasy is, simply stated, that you don't have to change anything about yourself in order to succeed in America. You don't even have to become an American.[30]

Stories of success and failure — of achieving or falling short of the dream — in America, in Hong Kong, and in many places, often center on the celebration and/or demonization of new arrivals. As the U.S. becomes just one destination of many for the Chinese diaspora and as more Americans find their way to Asia to travel, study, and work, the realities of globalization accelerate the movement of people, ideas, and capital across transnational space. Within a few years of *An Autumn's Tale*'s release, the rhetoric of Asian values would be squaring off against the post-Cold War exceptionalism of the American dream. The rhetorical battle was sidelined by crises on both sides of the Pacific. In the wake of the Asian financial crisis, Asian values (and the nations/quasi-nations who claimed that such values explained their economic success) took a beating as did the American dream after September 11, 2001. In the end, ideologies are, sometimes, altered by real-life events that challenge them and call for newer, more compelling explanations. However, the power of the American dream is not easily erased. Despite the events of June 4, 1989 and September 11, 2001, for many, a belief in the ability of the individual to adjust and succeed in an environment where certain freedoms exist is alive and well. In reality, as well as on screen, the notion of the dream may be damaged, but it is still compelling for many. *An*

Autumn's Tale holds out hope that the journey to new places is worth taking, and it is most worthwhile when people reach out to each other and refuse to exclude on the basis of labels such as "foreigner" or "immigrant."

Clearly, for many in diaspora, "happily ever after" is, indeed, just a dream. Cheung and Law acknowledge that in reality, Figgy did not actually transform into Samuel Pang. However, Cheung does believe certain opportunities do exist in the U.S. that are not available elsewhere. She declares that because of the difficulty of his life in China during the Cultural Revolution "real Figgy" chooses to "be satisfied with whatever he has" in the U.S. Even though he has learned how to perform certain aspects of American-ness, he will never become Americanized.[31] Endings are subject to individual interpretation and open to debate and cinema's conclusions present audiences with an opportunity to think more deeply about what lies beyond the fairy tale. The ending of *An Autumn's Tale* facilitates the beginning of many conversations. The film conveys an ambivalence about becoming an American that allows for the possibility of retaining a sense of belonging to Hong Kong/China and gently resisting the pull of overly idealistic American immigrant narratives. The characters in the film that are the least assimilated (and perhaps the most Chinese?) are also arguably the most "real" and appealing (Figgy and his buddies). Concurrently, those who are more Americanized (Mrs. Sherwood and Vincent) seem insecure and fickle.

The affirmation of Chinese-ness and a gentle reminder of the pitfalls of zealous assimilation/Americanization is a quiet but significant sub-theme within the film. In the process of rethinking the classic immigrant tale, a more nuanced appreciation for both home and adopted nations and cultures emerges. For scholars, students, and others who are interested in the "Here's Looking at You, Kid" gaze that global cinema casts on the U.S., *An Autumn's Tale* is much more than a romance. It is one of many film texts performing the cultural work of American studies from a perspective beyond the geographical borders of the U.S.[32]

One final anecdote about interpretations. When I told Cheung and Law that I wanted to discuss the film from the standpoint of transnational American studies they were intrigued but they also cautioned me not to "over-read" *An Autumn's Tale*. After all, Cheung insisted, the film is, first and foremost, "a small love story — a romantic comedy." Yet, after thinking a bit she added that in some respects the tale is actually larger than just the American dream. She asserts that the film is about "two people from different worlds coming together in New York City and figuring out how to love each other."[33] The discussion of New York City as an important space of "coming together" for the Chinese diaspora, is the subject of the next chapter.

5

A Tale of Two Cities:
New York in *An Autumn's Tale*

An Autumn's Tale takes us to a New York City that is, in the same instance, both familiar and foreign. On the familiarity front, audiences "know" certain New York City landmarks that appear in the film, such as the Statue of Liberty, the Brooklyn Bridge, Central Park, Battery Park, and Times Square. Cheung uses New York City landmarks, neighborhoods, modes of transport, and various urban spaces to move the plot forward and to illustrate how New York gradually becomes home for Jenny. This chapter argues that through the devices of narrative, style, and mise-en-scène, *An Autumn's Tale* engages the space of the city, as well as processes of border crossing in very deliberate — and familiar — ways. Audiences who see the film are reminded of other classic "American" books, plays, and films about newcomers trying to survive in New York. *An Autumn's Tale* is in conversation with other popular American movies made in and about the Big Apple. As a result, it addresses larger connections between cinema and urban space. Here again, we see links between film and transnational American studies as we note the way that New York is claimed as a familiar space by people from all over the world.

Manhattan is and has been a seemingly irresistible location for stories about the quest for upward mobility and achieving the American dream. New York is the setting for mid-20th century Broadway musicals turned cinema blockbusters such as *West Side Story* and *How to Succeed in Business Without Really Trying*. Although these productions promote the possibilities for success in America with tongue in cheek, they still strike a hopeful chord. Films about "making it" in the "city that never sleeps" have been standard fare for nearly a century and they experienced a resurgence of popularity during the late 1980s. In 1987, the same year *An Autumn's Tale* was released; Oliver Stone's *Wall Street* featured Michael Douglas as inside trader Gordon Gecko declaring "Greed is good." Like *Wall Street,* the *The Bonfire of the Vanities* (1990) both lampooned and seduced audiences with its depiction of life among Manhattan's financial elite.

Although the story of the business tycoon in Manhattan is a well-worn male narrative, there is a 1980s female equivalent — the tale of the upwardly mobile single woman. In this sense, *An Autumn's Tale* shares common ground with the Mike Nichols film *Working Girl*, starring Melanie Griffith, Sigourney Weaver, and Harrison Ford. Like *An Autumn's Tale* and *Wall Street*, it too was released in the late 1980s. *Working Girl* (1988) follows the fortunes of the young, perky, and independent (hereafter YPI) Tess McGill seeking success (and romance) in the big city. The fascination with YPI women "taking Manhattan" has not waned in the 21st-century and there seems to be a global market for stories of this sort. Films such as *Miss Congeniality, Maid in Manhattan, 13 Going on 30* and most recently, *The Devil Wears Prada*, continue to celebrate the YPI type, as do the ever-popular (globally distributed) re-runs of *Sex in the City* and *Friends*. Even reality television shows such as *America's Next Top Model* and *The*

Apprentice — among the hottest DVDs for sale in Shenzhen, China — reprise the theme.

Cherie Chung's character Jenny in *An Autumn's Tale* fits quite easily into the spunky sisterhood constituted by the women featured in the aforementioned films. Jenny is bright, idealistic, attractive, and willing to work hard despite the challenges the city presents. However, what separates Chung's Jenny from Meg Ryan's Sally, Melanie Griffith's Tess, or Anne Hathaway's Andy, is that *An Autumn's Tale,* like the film's Chinese title (literally "An Autumn's Fairy Tale") is a fantasy about life in New York for the young Chinese woman in diaspora. Jenny's quest is to find success and happiness in the city without losing her connection to her Hong Kong home or her Chinese-ness. This is a theme invoked in many Hong Kong films made in the 1980s and 1990s but Mabel Cheung Yuen-ting claims the space of New York City in *An Autumn's Tale* for diasporic women in a more Hollywood-like manner.

As a romantic fantasy, the story unfolds in a location that audiences everywhere know as a glamorous backdrop for myriad stories of success and hearts won and lost. Figgy and Jenny stroll through New York streets, riding in double-decker tourist buses, laughing in horse-drawn carriages, and flirting while watching/ playing baseball (Still 5.1). *An Autumn's Tale* evokes other New York cinematic romances from *Breakfast at Tiffany's* and *Barefoot in the Park* to *When Harry Met Sally* and *You've Got Mail.* The fairy-tale style reunion of Jenny and Figgy at the end of the film is not so distant from endings to classic New York cinematic romances such as *An Affair to Remember* or *Sleepless in Seattle.* As a Hong Kong director, Cheung stakes a claim in a space saturated by the Hollywood tradition of romance in Manhattan. As Jenny and Figgy saunter through various neighborhoods, blending into the crowds and falling in love in the process, they too claim the space of the city for themselves and for others who are part of the ever-growing Asian diaspora; to stroll, to love, to work, and to belong.

Still 5.1 *An Autumn's Tale*: Jenny and Figgy share a picnic atop a tourist bus as they ride along New York City streets.

By appropriating the Hollywood romance specifically for the diasporic soul, Cheung references a familiar genre and broadens its appeal for a more transnational moment. The classic "single girl in the city" story has a real-life resonance for increasing numbers of young women from many places in Greater China who find their way to New York (or other global cities) to visit, study, or work. While offering a glimpse into the difficulties of living in New York in a particular time period — the 1980s — the film nonetheless celebrates the possibility of happiness through reaching out to others in the complexity of urban space. Individual success is possible (in the film at least) because even when the city is cruel, there are friends nearby to make things right. *An Autumn's Tale* playfully critiques Ronald Reagan, self-absorbed 1980s "yuppies," and the tenor of the times, even as its sentimental shots of various New York City neighborhoods charm the viewer into believing that anything is possible.

In embracing the more idealistic side of the city, Cheung and Law eschew Hollywood's urban dystopias. This is not Gotham City, Dick Tracy's Manhattan, or Martin Scorcese's New York. Although

Jenny struggles to belong, she is initially distraught by Vincent's betrayal, and there are dark moments in the film (about which more will be said later), the city is, on balance, a place of adventure and self-revelation rather than violence and loss. In fact, the portrayal of New York in *An Autumn's Tale* differs from that of other Hong Kong directors who tell their own stories of Hong Kong women in Manhattan. The city featured in Clara Law's *Farewell China* or Stanley Kwan's *Full Moon in New York* is, in fact, more reminiscent of Scorcese. As Yingchi Chu notes, in *Full Moon in New York*, there are no images of famous landmarks or holiday decorations. "New York is represented as a cold, impersonal, lifeless and colorless city, a concrete jungle. The sky is foggy. Buildings stand side by side in the misty, hazy air. Canyons between buildings viewed from a low camera angle convey a feeling of oppression and depressing lifestyle."[1] In *An Autumn's Tale*, New York streets may be cluttered, but the clutter seems like actual stage scenery rather than real garbage. In nearly every outdoor scene the sky is blue (typical of some but by no means all New York City autumn days), and public spaces — even those that are cluttered with graffiti and rubbish — are inviting rather than foreboding (Still 5.2).

In some ways, Cheung's New York is, perhaps, a little closer to Spike Lee's depictions of urban life in films such as *Do the Right Thing* and *Crooklyn* where violence is an undeniable part of the story of life in the city, but a central preoccupation is the development of a range of characters and their relationships to each other as they navigate New York. It is people and their struggles with racism, economic hardship, and the daily demands (and joys) of family, friends, and employers that we see in both Cheung's and Lee's films. Like Lee, Cheung introduces us to a range of characters within a particular ethnic enclave, challenging stereotypes that circulate about minority groups in Hollywood films and in many places in U.S. society. Like Lee, who provides glimpses into the spaces and stories of African American communities in the city

Still 5.2   *An Autumn's Tale*: Scenes of New York are
sunny and inviting rather than dark and foreboding
as they appear in other Hong Kong diaspora films.

(and whose time at New York University's film school overlapped
with Cheung and Law's), Cheung facilitates glimpses into the
intimate spaces of Chinatown. In the process she is able to imbue
her Chinese and Chinese American characters with humanity as
she introduces us to a variety of narratives of migration, love,
striving and struggle.

Cheung and Law admire the work of many well-known
American/New York directors but they looked to one in particular
— Woody Allen — as they filmed *An Autumn's Tale*.[2] Allen and his
films are lovingly parodied in an exchange between Figgy and
Vincent in the Silver Palace Chinese Restaurant. Vincent tries to
convince Jenny that he is justified in running off to Boston with
another girl because, as Woody Allen has declared, "a relationship
is just like a shark, it has to keep moving." Figgy tells him that this
is "bullshit." Cheung and Law say they like the way Allen lampoons
the elite and "laughs at intellectuals" in his films.[3] Cheung's
cinematic take on New York in *An Autumn's Tale* is reminiscent of
Allen's *Manhattan* in several ways. She, like Allen, juxtaposes
diverse images of the city — romantic and artistic as well as gritty

and minimalist — with the dialogue flowing between characters. She also uses the sights and sounds of the city to signal transitional moments. Subway cars rumble by, ferry boats wheeze, and taxi horns bleat — signaling the beginning of a new scene, or an important event.

New York City as "Foreign"

While the film is clearly a romance, to focus only on the familiar, romantic, and idealistic side of Cheung's New York in *An Autumn's Tale* is to miss the ways that the city codes as "foreign" as well. Chinatown, literally blocks away from Wall Street, is, actually, a unique setting for the "girl in the city" tale. *An Autumn's Tale* introduces the audience to another side of Manhattan and is a reminder of less pleasant events that took place in the city during the 1980s. The film focuses on life in Chinatown during New York City's financial crisis. Figgy's sarcasm about the "trickle down" policies of the Reagan revolution in the 1980s serves as a reminder of the reach of shifting global economic trends and of domestic policy decisions made in Washington D.C. In one memorable scene, Figgy gives Jenny a ride to a babysitting job on Long Island. As they leave Manhattan in a battered convertible, twilight providing the backdrop for their journey, Figgy quips that he is proud of his car because after all, it is "just like Reagan's." *An Autumn's Tale* explores — albeit in a lighthearted manner — the various meanings of economic restructuring for newcomers from Asia who enjoyed a degree of wealth and prestige in their home cultures but experienced status loss and a slide into downward mobility in their daily lives in New York.

Not only is the city bewildering or unwelcoming in many ways for the newcomer from Greater China, the view of New York City itself, as seen through the camera, is, in some respects, a "foreigner's" view. As such, it can be somewhat disorienting. Those who know Manhattan and its environs can spot several places where Cheung and Law have taken liberties with certain details. For instance, Jenny is supposed to be landing at New York's John F. Kennedy Airport, but when she arrives she deplanes in the Newark, New Jersey Airport. She meets Vincent at the Lackawana Station but Vincent is coming from Boston. Trains from Boston are Amtrack trains and they arrive at Grand Central Station. In another scene Jenny boards a New Jersey transit bus for Long Island, something which is impossible to do as such buses shuttle people to and from New Jersey!

Part of the reason for the laxity about actual transport routes, and a mise-en-scène that appears, at times, somewhat contrived, is that the budget for *An Autumn's Tale* was only four million Hong Kong dollars (approximately half a million U.S. dollars). As this was the first feature film for Cheung and her second ever (the first being her thesis film) many of those involved in production were volunteers or beginners in the industry. Cheung and Law relied on "loyal friends from Chinatown" who acted as extras, helped with sets, and opened their shops for make-up and other production services because "everybody was crazy for Mr. Chow."[4] One actor in the film multi-tasked by working as a production assistant, and cooking for people on the set.[5] A cameraman convinced his mother to allow the cast and crew into her home to shoot the scenes in the Long Island home of Mrs. Sherwood and Anna. A makeshift grip was constructed and attached to a compact car both for convenience and economy. At the end of each day of filming all of the props were locked up in the same car. (One night after the film crew had dispersed, the most expensive prop — Jenny's watchband — was stolen.) Even Chow Yun Fat helped move sets (and was injured in the process). The total figure for salaries for the three leads in the film was less than HKD$600,000, and most of the other actors donated their time and labor. Predominantly New York-based, with the exception of a production assistant from Hong Kong, the crew was comprised largely of NYU graduate students or Cheung and Law's Chinatown friends. Cheung had only two months to make *An Autumn's Tale*. While the majority of the filming took place in New York City, the scenes with Jenny and Figgy inside their apartment building were filmed in Kowloon Tong, in Hong Kong. Post-production took place in Hong Kong as well.

There are moments where it is difficult to tell which scenes are intentionally styled and which look a bit rough around the edges due to crew inexperience and budget limitations. Consequently, the overall effect produced is somewhat odd. The city "looks" simultaneously familiar and foreign. Wide-angle shots of famous landmarks such as Times Square, Washington Square Park, and Central Park often zoom to close-ups that offer unexpectedly candid images of loneliness and melancholy. At night, as they walk through the Times Square area, Jenny and Figgy are hassled, jostled, or even jeered at by onlookers. As they stroll through the city streets past seedy movie theatres, pawn shops, all-night cafes and convenience stores, sirens blare and people stumble by (many of whom are drunk or disoriented, and, as noted in the last chapter, usually Black or Latino). In the early scenes, Jenny appears on the margins of the NYU campus, longing for acknowledgment from her peers. In her apartment we see her struggling to focus on her studies as the subway trains roar by her window shaking the table on which she is writing. New York is unwelcoming and New Yorkers seem cold and difficult to approach even though Jenny and other "outsiders" move freely past famous landmarks and tourist sites. Even streetwise Figgy — who professes not to care what others think about him — rarely ventures outside of his Chinatown cocoon. When he does, he too seems out of place.

One method for coping with the difficulties of adjusting to life in New York is to take refuge in the familiar. In *An Autumn's Tale*, food becomes an important barometer of belonging. The question of whether or not it is possible to eat well (read: eat like one would eat in Hong Kong) in New York is raised at several points throughout the film. The opening scene shows Jenny sitting on an airplane relishing the char siu (BBQ meat) that her mother insists on packing for her daughter because the flight is long and she will want to eat something besides airline food. A bit later in the film, a depressed and hungry Jenny stumbles into a Chinese restaurant to order lunch. She realizes that the only thing she can afford to order is a single-egg sandwich. Figgy happens to stroll by just as Jenny is about to begin eating her unappetizing repast. He sees her and saunters over to her table, greeting the owner of the restaurant who happens to be his friend. Figgy orders a proper meal for two (duck with rice, and bitter melon soup with extra melon — at no charge). He informs Jenny that "a country is only as good as its people and its people only as good as their food."

With this barb at the egg sandwich, clearly associated with American food — and a reminder of the "good" food and people she has left behind in Hong Kong — Figgy delivers a message to Jenny about the importance of staying close to her culinary and cultural roots. Throughout the film Jenny struggles to learn to prepare Chinese food in the U.S. Figgy tries to give her advice on how to cook properly, and although he doesn't seem to know much more than she does, his comments indicate his fondness for his mother's cooking, and the dishes he has known as a child. Food also becomes a source of alienation for Figgy later in the film when he visits an upscale Chinese restaurant where Jenny works as a hostess. Despite his knowledge of many types of local cuisine, Figgy cannot read the menu. He must rely on the waiter who orders an unfamiliar — and expensive — meal. Figgy appears glaringly out of place in the trendy restaurant, another reminder that New York beyond Chinatown is truly foreign for those who do not assimilate and learn to read as well as speak in English.

Like food, interior spaces within New York City carry symbolic weight in *An Autumn's Tale*. It takes time to make a home in New York, and it takes longer to make New York home. Jenny's Hong Kong flat is clean, sunny, and orderly, but her New York apartment is dirty, noisy, and dangerous. Cheung's use of lighting and camera angles inside Jenny's apartment set the stage for the darkest moment in the film, which takes place in Jenny's kitchen. Rejected by Vincent (Danny Chan), the boyfriend she has followed to New York, Jenny becomes despondent and lethargic. While she waits for water to boil to make a cup of coffee, she fails to notice that a gas leak is slowly filling the apartment with toxic fumes. The drip of the coffee pot on the gas range morphs into the foreboding sound of drums beating outside of Jenny's window, where there is a parade celebrating the Feast of San Gennaro. Merrymakers dressed as ghosts, skeletons, and other ghoulish figures dance along the street to the hypnotic beat. Images of the near hysteric celebrants are juxtaposed with Jenny crying, becoming drowsy, and eventually losing consciousness. Figgy, who lives in the apartment below, smells the gas and runs upstairs to rescue Jenny (Still 5.3). A crowd has gathered outside as firefighters break windows and seal off the building. The message conveyed here is that Jenny is not at home in New York. In fact, it is New Yorkers — dressed in festival attire — who appear foreign and exotic. As Figgy leads Jenny out onto the street for a bit of fresh air he must scream at the crowd waiting outside to "mind their own business." He is the "foreign other" pointing up the lack of civility among the New Yorkers gawking into the apartment building now ringed by fire trucks and emergency vehicles. Figgy protects Jenny from a New York City that is strange, poisonous, dangerous, and "other" from what she has known in Hong Kong. In the days following the fire, Figgy is more resolved in his determination to help Jenny claim the space of New York City as her own, which she will do by the end of the film. Subsequent scenes are filled with the couple transforming the apartment into a cozy domestic space, but we also see them struggle to feel secure in the city. Although each faces highly individual challenges, both must learn to survive in an impersonal environment where there is little daily comfort extended to them to cushion the difficulties they face.

Still 5.3   *An Autumn's Tale*: Figgy drags Jenny away from the toxic gas fumes filling her Chinatown apartment.

The Translocal in Transnational Space

As they navigate the sometimes familiar/sometimes foreign space of New York City, Jenny and Figgy appear to be in a world that is somewhere in-between Hong Kong and the U.S. Kwai-Cheung Lo notes that in many of the Hong Kong films made about migration in the 1980s, a Hong Kong-like space is reconfigured in various "foreign" cities. Citing films such as *Just Like Weather, Song of the Exile, Full Moon in New York*, and *Farewell China*, Lo argues that "the local is scrutinized in terms of its being displaced in different spaces and different times."[6] Figgy and Jenny become the embodiment of the "foreign" local. They are literally bodies displaced in different spaces and times. In *An Autumn's Tale,* there are moments in the film where audiences know the action is taking place in New York City, but the dialogue, characters, and surroundings look startlingly similar to Hong Kong. For instance, when Jenny walks into a diner in Chinatown, it is filled with people speaking Cantonese. Several of my students who watched this scene did not believe the action was truly being filmed in Manhattan. They saw dai pai dongs (local restaurants) that dot the streets of Kowloon.

The reconfiguration of the local in *An Autumn's Tale* is particularly apparent (and disarmingly endearing) when Chow's Figgy parodies "American-ness." One example of this occurs in the film when Figgy decides to take Jenny to a "Yankee Opera" (a Broadway show). He playfully mocks the character of the king in "The King and I" by placing a newspaper cap on his head and singing the first stanza of "Shall We Dance?" (This is a delicious bit of irony in light of the fact that over a decade later Chow would star in the remake of *The King and I, Anna and the King,* with Jodie Foster.) In a subsequent scene, the camera zooms from a wide-angle shot of Times Square to focus on Figgy, waiting in line with other tourists at TKTS, the discount ticket outlet in the Theatre District. Cold, impatient, and looking a bit bewildered by the number of people interested in "Yankee Opera," Figgy decides to jump to the front of the ticket line. In so doing he raises a few eyebrows but he does not seem to notice or care. Audiences can read this moment in two ways. On one hand, Figgy is conforming to the Hong Kong stereotype of the "backward" and somewhat clueless Mainlander from the PRC who doesn't understand the importance of lining up for tickets. Yet on the other hand, Figgy blends into the local scene as he is just acting like a New Yorker; somebody who knows that he has the inside track among the tourists waiting in line (Still 5.4). His assertiveness pays off and he does, indeed, manage to get the tickets.

Still 5.4   *An Autumn's Tale*: Figgy jumps to the front of the ticket line (angering or bewildering others) in order to purchase tickets for Jenny to see a Broadway Show.

However, Figgy's apparent ease negotiating the city turns to frustration once he learns that Jenny is unable to attend the Broadway play. As night falls he returns to the Times Square area where he stands in front of the theatre featuring the play he had hoped to see with Jenny. He is trying to re-sell the tickets to tourists passing in front of the box office, hoping he can get his money back. In this scene, Figgy again encounters the "foreign" New York, where his broken English and Chinese face mark him as an outsider and a potential troublemaker. A police officer accuses him of ticket scalping. Protesting that "I ain't no yellow cow" (an English translation of a Cantonese term for scalper) Figgy is unable to explain his situation. Jenny, who just happens to be passing by in a bus on the way to her babysitting job on Long Island, sees her frustrated friend from a distance (the sort of coincidence familiar to fans of romance films). She rushes to Figgy's rescue. As she approaches, she hears Figgy yelling in desperation at the police officer, "You talk all NO talk, I talk all YES talk."

Although Jenny does manage to diffuse the tension, the audience sees Figgy experience a type of shame reserved for those perceived to be outsiders or on the margins of the city. (The ease with which he had maneuvered his way to the front of the ticket line is now a distant memory.) Instead, we see Figgy's anger at the police officer turn to embarrassment as he becomes the outsider in need of rescue from Jenny — the newcomer he had hoped to impress with his knowledge of Broadway (Still 5.5). As Gina Marchetti notes, "while the cosmopolitan world of Hong Kong or New York promises a certain freedom associated with the hybridity of the metropolitan experience, it also represents a world in which identity is cast adrift, and there is no safe haven."[7] Chinatown becomes a place where Figgy's identity is stable. When he leaves his comfort zone and travels to the theatre district in mid-town Manhattan, Jenny comes to his aid, but also identifies him as an outsider. Figgy — in the eyes of the police officer — belongs to the seedier side of the Chinese diaspora.

Still 5.5 *An Autumn's Tale*: As the more fluent English speaker of the two, Jenny "rescues" Figgy from an altercation with a police officer.

For a number of reasons, among them social class, education, and level of English, Jenny's path to assimilation to America is less troubled than Figgy's. For her, the urban space of New York undergoes a transformation from lonely and dangerous to charming and welcoming. We witness Jenny evolve from being a despondent waif nearly asphyxiated in her apartment into a confident graduate student enjoying the acceptance of her peers at New York University. Although Jenny will, at the end of the film, choose to commute into Manhattan from the upwardly mobile suburbs of Long Island, she is "at home" in the city in ways that Figgy will never be. As she drives away from Figgy and the apartment building they have shared, autumn leaves dance with garbage in the streets. She literally leaves Figgy "in the dust." Figgy chases after the car but it is clear he will be left behind in Chinatown. (Cheung and Law laughingly reminisce about the way Chow Yun Fat and the film crew would run through the streets of lower Manhattan each day at sunset in order to shoot the dizzying montage of shots that make up the memorable penultimate scene.[8])

What happens next is, like the portrayal of New York itself in *An Autumn's Tale,* a final tale of two cities — foreign and familiar. Following a dizzying sequence of shots of the Brooklyn Bridge, the skyscrapers of lower Manhattan, graffiti-splashed cinderblock, transport signals, boats, subways, and taxis, the camera moves to a close-up of Figgy's crestfallen countenance. He sits looking forlornly at the watch Jenny has given him — the very watch that Figgy has sold his car for in order to purchase a watchband for her (Still 5.6). Julian Stringer has noted that in *An Autumn's Tale* and *Full Moon in New York* as well as *Rumble in the Bronx* the United States is, to borrow from Stuart Hall, "the third term" — "namely, a cultural space, neither Chinese nor European, where East meets West and new identities are negotiated."[9] Those new identities are often mediated by other factors making the city appear in a different light for various individuals. The third term/third space is very different for Figgy than it is for Jenny and we see that reality settle in as the camera pans out to show him sitting alone in the chilly twilight along the East River.

Still 5.6   *An Autumn's Tale*: Lower Manhattan at twilight provides the backdrop for Figgy's sadness at Jenny's departure.

As already noted, class differences allow Jenny to move out of Chinatown and economic hardship while Figgy will stay behind. In this respect, *An Autumn's Tale* points to deeper meanings of difference in the city as well as in diaspora. For Stringer, "part of the negotiation of issues of cultural identity and displacement in these films involves an exploration of the gap between the imaginative potential offered by travel to the new world and the humdrum fact of arrival."[10] It is the exploration of the gap — and the people one meets in the process of the exploration — that drives the narrative and makes the film significant for Cheung and Law, as well as for audiences who have viewed *An Autumn's Tale* over the past two decades.

As it does for Figgy and Jenny, New York City represents both the foreign and the familiar for Cheung and Law as well. They shared their own impressions of New York City during the 1980s as we discussed the making of *An Autumn's Tale*. Some stand out as particularly significant, and they mirror — to some extent — what audiences see in the film. During their graduate school years in New York City, they belonged to a cadre of pioneers who had the opportunity to meet and mix with Chinese Americans and people of Chinese descent from Taiwan, the PRC, as well as those from various socio-economic groups in Hong Kong. This was something they saw as both formative and historically significant because of the fact that relations with the Chinese mainland had been so recently normalized. As a meeting place for various Chinese populations, New York City offered a space where Chinese from Taiwan, Hong Kong, and the PRC could communicate freely. (While this was both liberating and interesting for those who shared the same urban space, Cheung and Law also note that various government organizations encouraged young Chinese students to spy on each other.) Contacts between individuals from various sub-ethnic groups living as members of the Chinese diaspora in New York were saturated with multiple meanings.

Another type of freedom that Jenny experiences in the film — and that Cheung says she experienced when she lived in New York — is the freedom from a particular past. At the beginning of the film, Vincent accuses Jenny of being a spoiled Hong Kong girl. However, by the end of the film, Jenny has learned to live on a very modest income. She is accepted by her peers at New York University and she appears comfortable mixing with a variety of people from diverse class and ethnic backgrounds in the city. Cheung, like Jenny, says she was impressed by the fact that so many of those around her were at liberty — to a certain extent — to remake themselves in New York. Protected by privilege in Hong Kong, Cheung is appreciative of the opportunity she had to meet and associate with Hong Kongers she would never have known had she not been a struggling single woman in New York. Speaking of the significance of this fact Cheung says:

In New York, you can make friends with other people with black hair, who speak the same language, and you forget that people's backgrounds are so different, and that some of them use foul language, or whatever, it doesn't really matter. They were all our friends — even triad guys — because Chinatown was so small. I worked in a video store and all of those mafia/triad guys came to my shop and they had to befriend me because they had to get certain episodes of TV series. If I became their friend I would save a particular episode for them. So they told me all kinds of stories about themselves. That's why we knew so many people from a very different class from us.[11]

A space saturated with meanings for film makers, moviegoers, and increasingly, new immigrants from Asia and elsewhere, New York City offers a site for border crossing on many levels.[12] Gina Marchetti underscores Cheung and Law's sense of the importance of the city for the Chinese diaspora, asserting that within Chinese communities in New York, "Chinese cultures from around the globe cross-pollinate, and what has been called 'transnational,' 'Greater,' or 'global' China emerges as a phenomenon that crosses national as well as cultural borders."[13] *An Autumn's Tale* offers a contemporary glimpse into a much older cross-cultural encounter.

Eclipsing the west coast "Gold Mountain" of the 19th century, the east coast is the 20th century symbolic heart of the new Chinese diaspora. Stringer declares that New York "is not just presented as a site for the allegorical disappearance of Hong Kong cultural identity. It also functions as a location for the mapping out of potential Asian American identities."[14] The New York stories told in Hong Kong films are not sparkling tales of lovers' reunions at the Empire State Building. Yet they do showcase the romantic spaces and New York City landmarks that have become familiar to the world, and they manage to invoke both a Hollywood and a Hong Kong sensibility. Additionally, because so many of those in the film industry move between New York and Hong Kong, they can celebrate and critique — often simultaneously — notions of home, nation, and identity within a well-traveled yet still often alien urban space. As both an American studies and a Hong Kong studies text, *An Autumn's Tale* serves as a reminder that at the end of the 20th century, mobility became the norm and home as a singular or plural locale became a place where the foreign and the familiar competed more profoundly than ever for the same domestic space.

6

Reconfiguring Gender in Diaspora

In this chapter, the focus shifts from transnational American studies, although the imprint of nation and national identity is still visible. Here *An Autumn's Tale* becomes a rich text to consider from a gender studies perspective. Recent work in transnational feminist/women's studies and men's/masculinity studies provides theoretical grounding for understanding multiple issues of gender and cultural identity in the film. Issues related to women and gender on screen and in light of connections to a larger Hong Kong/U.S. social context will be considered first. The second half of the chapter is a discussion of *An Autumn's Tale* in light of work in men's/masculinity studies. In its characters, plot, and ability to portray men and women evolving as more connected to each other in a new city, the film provides a strong counter narrative to Hollywood's orientalist portrayals of Chinese manhood and womanhood.

Women and Gender in *An Autumn's Tale*

In *An Autumn's Tale*, myths of romance and gender are reconfigured to suit the contemporary urban woman in diaspora. The film has more in common with the feel-good "have it all" romance *Working Girl* than the anti-feminist *Fatal Attraction* (both released the same year as *An Autumn's Tale*). In fact, as noted in the previous chapter, this Hong Kong take on the single girl in the city anticipates the "girl power" films that appeared a decade later — such as *Legally Blonde* and *Miss Congeniality* — as well as television series like *Friends* and *Sex in the City*. While it is not particularly heavy-handed about its message, *An Autumn's Tale* telescopes salient aspects of the process of gender and cultural negotiation for men and women in the postmodern metropolis and strikes a hopeful note about balancing personal and professional success.

As noted already, *An Autumn's Tale* is sunnier in its take on diaspora than other Hong Kong films made during the same period. Nowhere is this more clearly articulated than in various films' portrayals of women's experiences in New York. For example, in Evans Chan's *Crossings* a young Chinese woman is pushed onto the subway track by a spiteful American man who mistakes her for another "Asian" woman who has scorned him. In Clara Law's *Farewell China* an elderly woman asks a young husband searching for his wife: "Do you understand what it's like to be a woman all by herself in New York? Do you understand the desperation when there is menstruation and no money for sanitary napkins? Do you understand what it feels like to be raped?"[1] Men and women may share common ground in their respective adjustments to a new environment — both experience social or economic downward mobility or certain types of alienation for example — but there are important differences as well. As Gina Marchetti has written in her discussion of *Crossings*, "women experience a different type of "crossing" than men. Traditional roles for women dissolve in the diaspora. Families become unhinged, scattered; romantic relationships become more fleeting."[2]

But Marchetti also notes that the dissolution of traditional roles can bring freedom for women in new environments. Such is the case with Jenny. Although she is, at first, depressed by the fact that her boyfriend, Vincent, has left her for a more "American" girl, she learns to enjoy her independence. Initially, she relies on Figgy to help her navigate the city. In time she comes to enjoy living on her own in New York. *An Autumn's Tale* sends the message that women have choices and opportunities in diaspora. Compared to the women in *Crossings* and *Farewell China* (who are so alone that they experience dementia or become victims of violent crimes), Jenny's emotional baggage is almost non-existent.

In fact, as Jenny (Cherie Chung) travels along a quiet and unremarkable path to self-individuation in *An Autumn's Tale*, she is, actually, claiming a space in a well-established "girl power" tradition in Hong Kong cinema history, a history that pre-dates a similar phenomenon in the United States. Day Wong has shown that Hong Kong actresses who starred in film melodramas served as positive role models for a generation of young women coming of age in the 1960s. Wong argues that while women did not have "the discourse of women's liberation made available to them at that time," nonetheless, many women who watched Hong Kong melodramas "appropriated notions of female independence and sisterhood to resist the workings of patriarchal force." Film melodramas told stories that were "enabling rather than constraining, empowering rather than oppressive."[3] In the 1970s, Hong Kong television fulfilled a similar role. In fact, one particularly popular series featured Cherie Chung in the lead role. As Esther Cheung and Jamie Ku assert, "Television in the 1970s had produced many significant 'new woman' figures, many of which became collective memories of Hong Kong people who grew up at that time."[4] *An Autumn's Tale* continues a tradition of modeling how to be a successful, independent woman in a changing world, thus reflecting trends in Hollywood and Hong Kong.

Not only does *An Autumn's Tale* offer women a blueprint for survival and success in diaspora, it reflects a particular stance on gender and social change present in both the U.S. and Hong Kong during the 1980s and 1990s. That stance was a simultaneous embrace of certain aspects of the feminist project and a distancing from others. Although the 1980s is remembered as being a period of backlash against the feminist movement, 1987 (the same year *An Autumn's Tale* was released) was also the year of the Clarence Thomas/Anita Hill "he said/she said" sexual harassment episode. In fact, the discussion of women's status in the workforce was a constant source of discussion in newspapers, films, television programs and in homes and offices throughout the nation for much of the 1980s in the U.S.[5]

In Hong Kong, a nascent feminist consciousness was emerging in this period as women's issues dovetailed with broader public initiatives driving late-colonial democratic reforms. Yet, as Geetanjali Singh has noted, most Hong Kong women were/are keen to avert a full-on collision between the seemingly incompatible trains of tradition (or Asian values in 1990s parlance) and feminism.[6] Evelyn Ng and Catherine Ng remind us that Hong Kong women are conditioned to prize social harmony above other virtues.[7] Even avowed feminists know that they cannot afford to antagonize a conservative community with anxieties about the disruption of the uneasy but undeniable alliances between Confucianism, capitalism, and neocolonialism. It is not surprising, then, that artists and socially progressive Hong Kong citizens have learned to operate in "softly softly" mode — floating subtle rather than "in your face" calls for reform.[8]

An Autumn's Tale subtly illuminates the way myths about gender, sub-ethnic, and national identities are interwoven in cities where various groups who claim a Chinese identity live and work in close proximity. Jenny is compared with Vincent's new girlfriend who, at least in his eyes, is seen as more sexually liberated. "Over here girls are liberal minded," Vincent quips in rationalizing his choice of Chinese American Vivien over Jenny. Both women compete for Vincent's attention and it is clear that he can play each against the other to his advantage (Still 6.1). Jenny's insecurities about her physical appearance surface frequently throughout the film. She worries about not being pretty enough, or about being too old. When Figgy tries to reassure her that she should not worry about her age because he is a full decade older than she, Jenny retorts that "a 23-year-old woman is older than a 33-year-old man." The typical anxieties women feel about their looks in a culture obsessed by youth and beauty are amplified for newcomers who already feel marked as different.

Still 6.1 *An Autumn's Tale*: Vincent, literally "caught in the middle" of Jenny and Vivien, insists that American girls are "more liberal minded" and that Jenny — who has been in New York City for only a day — should follow suit.

The theme of women competing against each other surfaces in various ways in *An Autumn's Tale*. Chinese American women appear at several points in the film as troubled foils to Hong Kong womanhood as signified by the character of Jenny. In addition to Vincent's new girlfriend Vivien, Mrs. Sherwood and her daughter, Anna, who live in Long Island, are also Chinese American. Reminding the audience of how social class inflects gender and ethnicity, the film hints at how geographic distance from Chinatown translates not just into privilege but to a watering down of ethnic identity. Jenny may be a spoiled girl from the privileged neighborhoods of Hong Kong, but in New York City, she lives in squalor. The spacious house in Long Island is juxtaposed against Jenny's cramped apartment in Chinatown. Jenny is hired to tend Anna, but it is Anna who looks down on Jenny, despite her evident need for Jenny's "authentically Chinese" influence to help curb the excesses of Anna's Americanized behavior. Anna is a precocious (and demanding) child who tries to convince Jenny that her duties as a babysitter include peeling grapes. Jenny does not play Anna's game but works to give her the love and attention she needs because Anna's more "Americanized" mother is preoccupied with her career and her boyfriends.

Yet to focus too much on the tensions between women in *An Autumn's Tale* is to miss a more significant development. The film breaks ground in terms of telling an interesting and commercially successful story about women that neither patronizes nor orientalizes. As a response to stereotypes of Chinese women on American screens the film is significant on many levels, but two stand out as particularly noteworthy. First, Jenny is a refreshing departure from the Chinese women constructed as "suffering" heroines in the popular autobiographies circulating in the west at the end of the 20th century. As Christine So reminds us, these texts have institutionalized "the figure of the persecuted Chinese female expatriate, who emerges victorious and whole from the tumultuous, fragmenting, and dramatic events of the last century."[9]

Second, in its exploration of women's lives and the subtle (and not so subtle) references to differences between various groups of Chinese women in the United States, *An Autumn's Tale* is an important departure from Hollywood films where Chinese women have been and are, sadly, most often stereotyped as exotic and sexually available, deracinated, or controlling "dragon lady" types with thick, exaggerated accents. Neither victim, sex object, nor cartoon character, Jenny's struggle to belong seems less remarkable but more typical of a trajectory followed by thousands of women of the Chinese diaspora over the past century. *An Autumn's Tale* allows audiences to dream and romanticize without veering into caricature. In fact, the same argument can be made in terms of men and manhood in the film. It is to that subject, with a particular focus on Chinese masculinity as modeled through Chow Yun Fat's portrayal of Figgy in *An Autumn's Tale*, that we now turn.

An Autumn's Tale, Chow Yun Fat, and Chinese Masculinities

It is not just the women of *An Autumn's Tale* who reflect the complexities of gender role shifts occurring in New York and Hong Kong in the late 1980s. Chow Yun Fat's character, Figgy, is both an "old-fashioned guy" and a harbinger of change. In significant ways, the same can be said of Chow himself. To use a phrase coined in the 1980s, in real life, Chow is, according to Cheung and Law, a "sensitive new age guy." In *An Autumn's Tale* he quietly confounds many of the orthodoxies associated with his most famous Hong Kong film roles. Both Cheung and Law speak fondly of their collaboration with Chow and they readily acknowledge that a substantial portion of the film's success was linked to his presence.

Cheung was adamant that Chow be cast in the lead role. "Nobody had that kind of toughness mixed with romanticism ... He inspires romanticism." However, when they signed him to play Figgy, Chow's career was in a bit of a slump. Ironically, he agreed to star in *An Autumn's Tale* just hours before the Hong Kong premiere of *A Better Tomorrow*. Prior to the event, Chow joked that he was "box office poison." However, *A Better Tomorrow* was so successful that had Cheung and Law waited another day — or even a few hours — to sign him, they would not have been able to afford to pay the salary he could command.[10]

Like his character in *An Autumn's Tale*, Chow knows what it is like to be between cultures and worlds. Although he spends a significant amount of time in Hollywood and is well known to film fans in Asia and the west, Hong Kong people claim Chow as their own. Born in 1955 on Lamma Island, near Hong Kong, Chow's family was poor and he had to quit school at seventeen to work several odd jobs (messenger, salesman, bellboy, cab driver). He began his career with a local Hong Kong television station, TVB, where he spent nearly 14 years acting in various series. He earned significant fame for his starring role in the soap opera *Shanghai Bund*.[11] Julian Stringer notes that Chow made an easy transition to the big screen and to fame. While he won international awards and became famous for his roles in gangster/cop thrillers, he also appeared in smaller, independent films like Ann Hui's *Love in a Fallen City* (1984) and Stanley Kwan's *Love Unto Waste* (1986). "What holds the range of such roles together," Stringer says, "are his good looks, easy charm, and a slippage between his being both totally in and totally out of control.[12]

Clearly, however, Chow is best known for his roles in John Woo films such as *The Killer* and *A Better Tomorrow I* and *II*. Stringer, who has explored the topic of Chow's portrayal of various models of Chinese masculinity in Hong Kong cinema, argues that despite the "masculinist" and "patriarchal" aspects of *The Killer* and *A Better Tomorrow,* "they do seem to recognize the instabilities within a historically specific conception of patriarchal masculinity."[13] This is important because Chow has played a significant role in helping to refashion the way Chinese men are seen on screen and in daily life in various parts of the world. This is no small task. As Sheridan Prasso writes, the majority of characters played by Asian men in Hollywood "have been small, sneaky, and threatening — or spineless, emasculated wimps, or incompetents who may well be technically proficient in martial arts, but impotent when faced with white man's superior strength or firepower." Not only does this mean that "they almost never get the girl," but even more disturbing, "what we see of Asian male sexuality is the assertion of a stronger Western virility at the expense of Asian masculinity."[14] Chow's characters counter the stereotypes that Prasso and scholars in Asian American and Hong Kong cultural studies have critiqued. Known for being both tough and vulnerable on screen (and for being a filial son who still shops for food in local wet markets and cooks for his aging mother on a regular basis), Chow enjoys idol-like popularity among the diaspora, yet his characters generate an intense discussion of manhood and Chinese culture in many settings.

In the past decade, as scholars in several fields — Asian studies, Asian American studies, Hong Kong cultural studies, and masculinity/men's studies — have discovered Hong Kong films and film stars, the conversation about men, gender, and masculinity on screen has been enriched. Chow Yun Fat is just one of several Hong Kong leading men (others include Bruce Lee, Jackie Chan, Jet Li, and Stephen Chow), who have become subjects of serious study. Chow's performance in *An Autumn's Tale* does indeed talk back to Hollywood's orientalist stereotypes of Chinese men as inscrutable, emasculated, or hypermasculinized warriors. However, as Laikwan Pang and Day Wong have noted, it is important to look at the range of masculinities on display in Hong Kong cinema and to pay attention to diverse genres within the industry. Although certain roles or movies are seen as representative of the genre or a particular star, the reality is that there has always been a range of films, leading men, and masculinities on display in Hong Kong cinema. Pang also reminds us to "read more carefully the nuances and complexities of these male representations within their historical context to investigate how they produce different, or often unstable, meanings of maleness."[15]

Reading *An Autumn's Tale* through the lens of recent research in men's/masculinity studies offers the chance to consider Chow's character, Figgy, in light of models of masculinity in the U.S. and in Hong Kong during the late 1980s. The film is dramatically different from the Chow/John Woo heroic bloodshed pas de duex, or the Hollywood films of the period (such as *Die Hard* and the *Lethal Weapon* and *Rambo* series). As Susan Jefford notes, many of these films showcase the male hard body and represent the Reagan-era appetite for national as well as individual masculine strength. *An Autumn's Tale* celebrates a different kind of strength. Figgy's (Chow's) machismo is actually informed or even trumped by his capacity to care for Jenny.[16]

In fact, *An Autumn's Tale* is not the only film to feature Chow as a sensitive hero. On global screens, he may be best known as the star of John Woo's Hong Kong films. But, as Kwai-Cheung Lo has noted, that is because western viewers have limited opportunities to see the range of roles that Chow portrays as he is so often forced to play "generic and flat Chinese characters."[17] *An Autumn's Tale* is one of many Hong Kong films that feature Chow's ability to move beyond the warrior stereotype. In the process, he illustrates Kam Louie's notion of the Wen/Wu model of Chinese masculinity which challenges Hollywood's caricatures of emasculated or hyper macho archetypes. Louie notes that, "Hong Kong (and its derivative Hollywood) films are ideal sites for unmasking Chinese masculinity in a global context."[18]

Chow's performance as Figgy also manages to talk back to stereotypes of Chinese American men both on Hollywood screens and in U.S. society at large. Robert Lee has noted several problems with depictions of Chinese men in U.S. movies. For much of Hollywood's history it was common to cast white actors as Chinese, reproducing Yellowface performance even after Blackface was considered unacceptable. Even when Chinese men are cast as Chinese characters, stereotypes remain intact. Sadly, in addition to the "absolute Oriental Otherness" of early Hollywood caricatures of the cunning villain, Fu Manchu, or the noble but inscrutable Charlie Chan, more recent Hollywood representations of Chinese/ Chinese American men have not improved significantly.[19] As King-kok Cheung has asserted, one cannot overlook "the historically enforced 'feminization' of Chinese American men." She urges a closer look at "the dialectics of racial stereotypes and nationalist reactions" and the importance of "wrestling with diehard notions of masculinity and femininity in both Asian and Western cultures" in order to move beyond stereotype.[20] *An Autumn's Tale* does not really wrestle with "diehard notions of masculinity and femininity," yet it does quietly push at convention as it tracks Jenny's quest to be independent and Chow's efforts to nurture her.

"A Real Man Doesn't Say Someday, He Says Today": Gender in Diaspora

Chow portrays the role of the typical "white knight" in *An Autumn's Tale* by rescuing Jenny from the danger of the city. Yet, in other ways, Figgy is atypical. He doesn't just save Jenny. He takes care of her in stereotypically "feminine" ways. He teaches her how to cook authentic Chinese food, he shows her how to make her cramped apartment a real home, and, although he does not speak "proper" English or have much education, he helps Jenny see the importance of taking her own schoolwork seriously. He admonishes, "Study hard, and don't let people look down on you." In the film, he makes it clear that it is, actually, quite "manly" to help her in these ways. When they discuss the best time for him to come and build a bookshelf for her apartment, Jenny is concerned that he not feel rushed to complete the task. But Figgy replies, "A real man doesn't say someday, he says today. Let's go after this."

Yet even as Figgy assumes these stereotypically feminine tasks, he continues to carry on gambling and picking fights with rival gangs (Still 6.2). As previously noted, because he comes from a different socio-economic class than Jenny, and he doesn't speak English confidently, he is clearly on the margins of the city. He maintains close ties with his gambling buddies, and he exhibits a certain level of machismo even as he mothers Jenny. It is, in fact, Figgy's gambling and gang fighting that alienates Jenny to the point where she decides to leave the city. However, Figgy is, in many respects, the most responsible character in the film. He takes care of those around him and he is unfailingly loyal and protective of those who are important to him. He is, consequently, admired by those he works to help in daily life.

Still 6.2 *An Autumn's Tale*: Figgy and his friends end up in a gang fight as a result of Figgy's (mis)reading of Vincent's reappearance in Jenny's life.

Figgy's masculinity is complex. He may be a man of influence in terms of being able to order free food for himself and his friends in Chinatown restaurants, but he is looked down upon by wealthier members of the diaspora. He realizes (and jokes about the fact that) the Reagan revolution has passed him by, and he works as a busboy in the Silver Palace Restaurant to supplement his income as a building manager in Jenny's apartment complex (and to pay his gambling debts). After leaving his own birthday party because he fears Jenny is going to reconcile with Vincent, Figgy bets (and loses) his last $600. Walking out of the gambling den he declares, "All cleaned out! No money, No worry!" When he returns briefly to his apartment and Jenny asks him where he is going, Figgy's friend replies, with a double entendre response, "Nowhere." Near the end of the film Jenny asks Figgy to come and visit her after she is settled in her new home on Long Island. Figgy promises her he will do so, "someday." The two of them share a poignant moment as they reflect on a similar conversation several weeks earlier when he told her that a real man never says someday, he says today. What goes unsaid in the exchange is that Figgy is not yet a "real man." Is manhood then, ultimately tied to economic success?

Despite a certain immaturity, as an individual who makes a positive difference in the lives of his friends, and who eases Jenny's transition to the U.S., Figgy is indeed successful. *An Autumn's Tale* endows the marginalized diasporic man with humanity. Not only does Figgy stand in contrast to the "preppy" Vincent or Mrs. Sherwood's womanizing boyfriends, he represents a cohort of men who are left behind as the U.S. economy completes a difficult transition into post-industrial gear. The phrase "capital is theft" is prominently spray-painted on the wall of the apartment building where Jenny and Figgy live. He may be the underdog in terms of his earning power but he is the strongest and most honorable of the men in the film. The audience cannot help but simultaneously ache and cheer for Figgy. Thanks to Chow's acting ability, Figgy is charming rather than threatening. One wonders if his real-life counterpart was as cavalier about his downward mobility during the difficult economic shifts of the 1980s.

Returning once more to Kam Louie's notion of the Wen/Wu hero as somebody who manifests both physical strength and an intellectually grounded tenderness, note that Louie sees Chow Yun Fat as the embodiment of the ideal. Chow does, after all, display many types of behavior in his various film roles. Louie argues that Chow's characters are linked to a long history of diverse (and underappreciated) models of manhood in Chinese culture. Chow models both Wen (a more scholarly, mental, or civilly-minded type of masculinity) as well as Wu (the martial or physical type of masculinity). "Because it captures both the mental and physical composition of the ideal man, Wen-Wu is meant to be constructed both biologically and culturally," Louie argues.[21] In *An Autumn's Tale*, although the Wen-like wisdom he shares is more homespun than erudite, Chow's Figgy is a thoughtful character who constantly tries to teach as well as to help Jenny. There is no doubt that his Wu side defends Jenny's honor and his friend's business venture by engaging in street fighting. Yet Figgy is still comfortable enough in his masculinity to help Jenny remodel and decorate her apartment. Because he is so well-known (in many cases beloved) among the diaspora, there is an intertextuality between Chow the man and Figgy the character. Chow as Figgy offers audiences an alternative to cinematic models of manhood so prevalent in both Hong Kong and Hollywood. Figgy may be less economically successful than the other men in the film, but he manages to display a more sensitive range of masculine behaviors that Jenny (and the audience) ultimately finds appealing.

Julian Stringer offers another explanation for Figgy's enlightened masculinity. Perhaps his ability to care for Jenny has more to do with downward mobility than gender bending. Stringer asserts that while Jenny wants to see the world, Figgy wants to stay put and open a restaurant. This is not because he lacks ambition but rather because "he is structurally excluded from New York's capitalist miracle, and he has no white friends." However, "by offering a highly tentative fantasy in its very last moments, the film suggests that Sam Pan may yet come to embody an alternative paradigm of Asian American identity."[22] Stringer reminds us that although *An Autumn's Tale* is a romance, there is a dark underside to the seemingly happy tale, particularly for men like Figgy, who are seen as expendable in the ebb and flow of the new economy.

Keeping Stringer's reading in mind, however, Chow's Yun Fat's characterization of Figgy is still important for two reasons. First, the film offers a genuine alternative to the model of masculinity proffered by Hollywood's "Chinese men." (In fact, the mere presence of a range of Chinese men playing themselves is a relatively recent development in Hollywood history.) Second, *An Autumn's Tale* engages issues related to masculinity for Chinese as well non-Chinese men. In that respect, the film plays a small part in the effort to (in the words of King-Kok Cheung) "reclaim cultural traditions without getting bogged down in the mire of traditional constraints, to attack stereotypes without falling prey to their binary opposites, to chart new topographies for manliness and womanliness ..."[23] I am not arguing that Figgy is the ideal man because he can both gamble and clean house. That merely makes him a SNAG of another sort — a sensitive new-age gambler. Rather, Chow's portrayal of Figgy serves as a reminder that there are compelling portraits of masculinity in Hong Kong film, that in some cases Hong Kong film serves up alternatives to the standard portrayal of manhood a la Hollywood, and that even a romantic melodrama like *An Autumn's Tale* offers a point of departure for a conversation about broadening the parameters of gender to make way for a range of desires, talents, and contributions.

Unfortunately, while Louie, Cheung, and others point to alternative models of masculinity, the Hollywood stereotypes die hard. Despite the success that Hong Kong film stars such as Chow, Jackie Chan, and Jet Li have enjoyed in the U.S. (and on global screens), their popularity abroad has, to a certain extent, meant less, not more open discussion of new ways of being masculine. Wai-Kit Choi writes of the paradox of the "co-existence of multiculturalism and cultural domination." While artists such as John Woo and Jackie Chan may depart from traditional masculinities in their early careers, once they migrate to Hollywood, "their alternative representation of masculinity becomes assimilated into the mainstream American system of male representation." For Wai, this shows "how Hollywood manages multiculturalism and maintains the hegemony of a representation schema that subordinates the other."[24]

One might argue that Chow Yun Fat has managed to keep his characterizations of men and masculinity — Chinese or otherwise — at a relatively nuanced level, despite his success outside of Asia. However, there is in *An Autumn's Tale* an ease and a charm that one does not always see in his crossover/Hollywood films. Arguably, Chow's most compelling performances are those most closely associated with his Hong Kong roots. The textured masculinity he exhibits in *An Autumn's Tale* supports this assertion. One can only hope that regardless of where home is for Chow, he will continue to portray a range of roles (and types of masculinity), even as he enjoys increased success on global screens (Still 6.3).

Still 6.3 *An Autumn's Tale*: An ebullient Figgy runs through the streets of New York City, anxious to see Jenny and present her with the watch band he has purchased for her.

7

Conclusion:
An Autumn's Tale in 2007

Two decades after its release, *An Autumn's Tale* remains, in the minds of many, a Hong Kong cinema classic. In addition to recognizing its staying power and popularity with a multi-generational fan base, the film merits an even more prominent place in the discussion of the Hong Kong New Wave/Second Wave. *An Autumn's Tale* sheds light on a particular time (the late 1980s) and a particular historical phenomenon (the "brain drain") in an easy yet profound manner. In addition, the film is a rich text for engaging the topics explored in the previous chapters such as: Connections between Hong Kong film and transnational American studies; between Hong Kong and Hollywood films about/set in New York; and, between Hong Kong film and recent work in gender studies. The film also serves as a bridging text between Asian studies, Hong Kong cultural studies, Asian American studies, and transnational American studies.

There is another reason to take a fresh look at *An Autumn's Tale* two decades on. As I write this conclusion, Mabel Cheung

Yuen-ting's classic is making headlines in both the Chinese and English press. A daytime screening of the film, aired on a local Hong Kong television station in October of 2006, stirred up a bit of controversy. A parent, who was disturbed about the graphic language used in the film, lodged a complaint with Hong Kong's media watchdog, the Broadcasting Authority (BA). The BA declared that *An Autumn's Tale* contained "extremely offensive expressions" and they ruled to ban it from being aired on local television stations.[1]

The outcry from the public was immediate and near unanimous in its support for overturning the ban and allowing the film to be shown during prime time. Mabel Cheung Yuen-ting and Alex Law were both bewildered by the ruling. They continue to maintain, as they noted in both of my interviews with them, that one purpose of making *An Autumn's Tale* was to promote understanding between various individuals and diverse groups of people in a foreign place. The language is mild by any standard (particularly in comparison to what passes as acceptable language on most channels on a daily basis in Hong Kong). Additionally, there was a parental guidance warning posted before the film aired. Cheung says she understands that parents want to protect their children from danger but she thinks it would be best to "let children get in touch with all kinds of people."[2] The incident is a reminder of the strange morality that governs Hong Kong in its incarnation as a Special Administrative Region of the PRC. In a *South China Morning Post* editorial, Chris Yeung wrote, "The broadcasting watchdog's ruling has raised the question of whether government appointees have a grasp of what is acceptable to TV viewers. Is Hong Kong truly a modern, progressive world-class city?"[3] Yeung's comments are a fitting end to this study of *An Autumn's Tale* for it was anxiety about a loss of freedom that drove so many "Jennys" and "Figgys" away from Hong Kong in the 1980s. Those who are interested in the cycles of history, (as well as finding out what all of the fuss is about), might want to pick up a copy of *An Autumn's Tale* and make up their own minds.

Appendix

Interview with Mabel Cheung Yuen-ting and Alex Law

Interview conducted by the author with Mabel Cheung Yuen-ting and Alex Law in the University of Hong Kong Senior Common Room, Monday, June 26, 2006.

SF: It's been 20 years since *An Autumn's Tale* was released. Two decades later, what do you think about the film?

Cheung: It's a very honest film and it's one of our very early films. It's about our friend, who is "Sam Pan" (Samuel Pang) in the film. He's actually based on a friend of ours in Chinatown. I think technically, it might not be the best of our films, but in terms of energy I think it is memorable — one of our most memorable.

SF: How long were you in New York?

Cheung: We were there for our Master's Degrees (at NYU, beginning in 1982).

Law: We were there for the degree for three years, but since that time we've gone back on and off. Almost every year we'd go back to see our friends, or to see the place, or just to be there.

SF: So you spent most of the 1980s either living in or traveling back and forth from New York City. It was a time of economic difficulty and the city was much different then than it is today.

Cheung: Now it's much tidier — and cleaner — but I liked the eighties.

SF: Were there other "New York" film directors who inspired you?

Cheung: Of course I loved Martin Scorsese and also Woody Allen. And back then Woody Allen said that the only cultural advantage in L.A. was that you could turn right on a red light so he said he would never go there to shoot a film. He was a New Yorker and was going to be in New York all the time ... He hated palm trees ... and that's what I thought too back then ... I had never been to L.A. ... so I thought, oh yes, New York's the best city in the world, I have to make films here.

SF: Alex, what do you think about the city? Do you share that view?

Law: I love the city. Actually I love it better the old way. It was a little bit dirty, a little bit dangerous, but very, very exciting. Every day was like a roller-coaster ride ... and almost every month, either we ourselves, or our classmates, or somebody we knew would lose something, or something would be stolen from us — or we would see crazy people on the street — but it was all very inspiring.

Cheung: In Hong Kong I studied at Hong Kong University. While I was here I never had the chance to get to know certain people — like the tough guys in Mong Kok. I would never go to Mong Kok and befriend the tough guys because I had my family and friends in Hong Kong surrounding me and I was in a world of my own. But in New York I had no money and I had to work part-time in Chinatown because the school fees were so expensive and living in New York was really beyond my means, so I really had to befriend all of those Chinatown tough guys.

SF: How did you two meet?

Law: We met in class. At that time there were only three of us who were Chinese ... Both of us and one guy from Taiwan.

Cheung: I think maybe there are more Asian faces now but we were the only three and before that there was only Ang Lee.

Law: He (Ang Lee) was there during that famous ten-year period, hanging around.

Cheung: And Spike Lee was there too, and the two Lees lived together as "minorities" in Alphabet City. That's where we shot one of our student films.

SF: The question of autobiography arises when talking about this film. Is this your story? Do you see the character of Jenny [Cherie Chung] in you?

Cheung: Jenny's experience (like in the egg sandwich scene) was my experience too because we really were broke and we could only afford an egg sandwich with just one egg. That was our story. Sometimes we had to walk from NYU to Chinatown to our workplace in the wintertime and it was a forty-five minute walk in the wind and snow.

Law: Back then when we wanted to go to Lincoln Center to see a movie or whatever, we also had to walk eighty blocks. And after 1984, the Hong Kong dollar dropped in value so much that we lost half of the money we needed for our school fees. There were no scholarships for overseas students.

SF: I confess, when I first saw the film, I figured the script had been written by a woman. Alex, how were you able to create a character (Jenny) who is so authentic?

Law: Because I know her [Yuen-ting]. Actually, in the very first draft, the original idea was a story about a relationship between a male student and a Chinatown "bum." And when we presented the idea to the studios they said, nobody is going to watch a film like this — about the friendship between two guys — much less between a student and a Chinatown "bum." So we changed it to a Chinatown "bum" and a Hong Kong girl. That was stage two of the development of the story.

Cheung: But then they asked us to change that too. They said nobody would be interested in a Chinatown "bum" — because only maybe three thousand people had gone to New York — so they recommended we change the character to a Mong Kok "bum" and a Hong Kong U[niversity] student. I said, that in Hong Kong it doesn't work, because a Hong Kong female student would never go to Mong Kok and she doesn't have to depend on that guy. She has other friends.

Law: She wouldn't be so stranded like she was in a strange land. In Hong Kong, she could always go home, or go to her friends.

SF: So it's being in a new place that erases some of those boundaries between people?

Cheung: In New York, you can make friends with other people with black hair, who speak the same language, and you forget that people's backgrounds are so different, and that some of them use foul language, or whatever, it doesn't really matter. They were all our friends — even triad guys — because Chinatown was so small. I worked in a video store and all of those mafia/triad guys came to my shop and they had to befriend me because they had to get certain episodes of TV series. If I became their friend I would save a particular episode for them. So they told me all kinds of stories about themselves. That's why we knew so many people from a very different class from us.

SF: The film was quite commercially successful and some critics dismissed it as a result. What do you think about the commercial success of the film?

Cheung: It was not meant to be a commercial success ...

Law: It was a surprise.

Cheung: And when we made it we went to all the major studios. They all said no because first, it's not a major mainstream story. Second, it's called *An Autumn's Tale*, which sounded strange in Chinese.

Law: A little bit too arty, too literary ...

Cheung: And third, we wanted to use Chow Yun Fat who was — back then — box-office poison ...

SF: Why was he seen that way?

Law: He'd made quite a number of films and they all flopped. But it's funny, at that time we were all sitting around talking late one evening and we asked him if he'd be interested in doing the film and he said, "Of course. I'm box-office poison anyway, so yeah, I'm glad to be part of it." And then half an hour later we all went to the midnight screening of *A Better Tomorrow*. We went together. We were sitting on the steps (because there were no seats available) the three of us ... and it was such a big, big hit. We were so glad that we talked to him beforehand.

SF: What was it like working with him? Had you worked with him before?

Cheung: We knew him from a film he had been in which he [Alex] wrote.

Law: You'll like the title ... It's called *A Hundred Ways to Murder Your Wife* (Laughter). It was a crazy, harmless comedy, and we became friends. He didn't really care about his own stage presence or screen presence; he'd just do whatever you wanted him to do — a very nice guy to work with.

Cheung: Chow said he was really excited to go and work in New York but then all of the big bosses whom I took the story to asked if we could change the male lead and they suggested other big stars like Michael Hui who was [back then] a bigger star ...

Law: They were almost going to give us Jackie Chan, but they said if it was Jackie Chan then of course the girl would fall for him anyway. We insisted on Chow which was one major reason why we were turned down by so many major studios because we said it has to be Chow Yun Fat.

Cheung: Nobody had that kind of toughness mixed with romanticism ... He inspires romanticism. I talked to Chow and told him that I'd been turned down by this studio and that studio and he said, "I know, I'm not a big star ... "

Law: Very sweet ... very nice guy.

SF: So it was a surprise when it was a commercial success. Who was surprised?

Cheung: Everybody was surprised, even the boss ... He had only booked two weeks for show time. After that, the theatres had to make room for the screening of the Disney cartoon, *An American Tale*. But at the end of the second week it was still making half a million dollars a day and they could not take it off the screen and my producer, John Sham, who protected us all the time and who fought for the film to be made ... He was furious because the boss had signed away theatre space to *An American Tale* and there was no way he could break the contract so he personally asked around for other cinemas to show the film.

SF: How did the film do outside of Hong Kong?

Cheung: I think it did quite well. It was shown in a lot of film festivals. Back then there was no distribution network. There was a Chinatown distribution network, of course, and all over the world it was a great box office success among the diaspora. It was a surprise to everybody. In Japan too it was a great success. I really do not understand the success of the film, it was beyond my imagination. The only problem was that afterwards, everybody asked me to do the same kind of film over and over again and that's why I tried to make *The Soong Sisters* which was completely different. *An Autumn's Tale* opened a lot of doors for me. My name was recognized.

Everywhere we went people would come up to us and offer us a cup of tea. It was an amazing phenomenon. And Chow became a big star afterwards. Of course by the time the film was released, he was already a big star, and that helped. So I was really surprised. I know that some critics say that if a film is a commercial success, then artistically, it must be a failure. But I don't think so. I want the film to be seen by a lot of people. I went to the cinema and watched these lines queuing around the cinema and I was happy.

Law: There's a mentality with a lot of Hong Kong film critics. Somehow if a film makes it big commercially then they think it must be a trashy film. They don't really believe in a film that is critically acclaimed, and also commercially successful.

SF: Do you think that other filmmakers who came later were influenced by your film? Is there a link between *An Autumn's Tale* and films like *Farewell China, Full Moon in New York,* or *Comrades: Almost a Love Story*?

Cheung: People influence people and we were influenced by other people, so it doesn't really matter. Looking back, I think that *An Autumn's Tale* was really different from the films being made at that time. Back then we had films like *Police Story*. It was a time when action film and comedy were big in Hong Kong. So this film, when it came out, was really fresh and honest because it was from our experience, and it was about our friend whom we loved. Of course there were many parts of the film that were fictional, but we really loved this friend and he was our lifetime friend.

SF: Is he still alive?

Cheung: Yes ... but he doesn't have a restaurant.

Law: And what happened afterwards was not so rosy.

Cheung: Yes, in real life, it was so sad. He went to prison and he was betrayed. But in the film, as a director, I could give him a restaurant ... I am the creator of this film so I insisted. At that time there was a difference of opinion about the ending. My producers said to me you can end with the scene where they parted and Chow Yun Fat is standing underneath the bridge looking at the watch. But I felt like I wanted to give a restaurant to my friend.

Law: But at the time we made the film, he was still living there [in New York]. Whatever else happened to him happened after we were finished shooting. It's a sad story. But he was there, and he helped us build the Sam Pan Restaurant by the waterfront. And what's funny is that when I went there, I looked at the set and I said to myself, hey, there's a spelling mistake here. It doesn't say Sam Pan, it says Sam Man. And it was him, he'd made the sign ... But I thought I shouldn't change it. After all, it's him ... he was the kind of guy who would spell his name wrong. If you look at the film again you'll see that it says Sam Man not Sam Pan.

Cheung: That was just his way of talking, he'd speak very fast, fluent, English but it was all 'wrong' ...

SF: In some ways this is a historical story about how "outsiders" are marginalized in the U.S. but by the end of the film, they are Americans. Because it is a romance, it becomes a story about how people can "fit" although they still face difficulty and discrimination. It is also a story about Hong Kong and the "brain drain" (the exodus of many people between the signing of the Joint Declaration in 1984 and the resumption of Chinese sovereignty in 1997). I see it as an important bit of history as well as a story. How do you feel about that?

Cheung: Do you know why we made the *The Illegal Immigrant*? Because at that time, particularly at that point in history, everybody was interested in immigrating. All of my friends after the 1983 meeting where Margaret Thatcher tripped in front of the Hall of the People ... All of my friends in New York were thinking of different ways of "staying over" ... including arranging fake marriages. We were all thinking we shouldn't go back to Hong Kong because we were all so uncertain about the future and we were so afraid of the Communist Party. And we had to go back to a Motherland who was completely strange to us and we were strange to them too. We were like adopted children. So that's why we were obsessed with immigration in our films. You are right. I think maybe subconsciously we are all influenced by history and by the things that happen to us at that particular point in time. I didn't consciously say, "Wow, this is such a historical moment and I have to make a film about it." But looking back, it kind of documents the experience of that time and the psychology of the people at that point in history and also the people in Chinatown who came to live there. It's like a shelter for the Chinese people who do not speak English because there were lots of illegal immigrants after the Cultural Revolution who jumped ship and stayed in the United States and that's the background of Sam Pang too. He escaped from China during the Cultural Revolution. That was the true background of our friend. He escaped to Hong Kong and then he became a sailor and as a sailor he went to New York and then he jumped the ship and stayed in New York as an illegal immigrant. And that's also the story of a lot of his friends. His whole group of friends were also of that same background. But they stayed in Chinatown and pretended that they were in China. Every day they'd wake up and go to Chinese restaurants and eat the same Chinese food, and they'd speak Chinese. They never had to speak a word of English because everybody in Chinatown speaks Chinese. They gamble and they work in Chinatown. Actually, they seldom go out.

SF: But you do move the story out of Chinatown with the mother and daughter on Long Island. Did you think about the fact that you were looking at different groups both in and out of Chinatown?

Cheung: Actually, I was somewhere in between. I worked in Chinatown part time but then I studied at NYU which was further uptown and all of my classmates were white and some of my Chinese middle-class friends lived on Long Island. They had been in America since the 1970s. Many of them had studied in America and had become very Americanized ... They had American boyfriends, and they tried not to go into Chinatown. It's a very strange psychology that this group of middle-class Chinese Americans demonstrated. They had studied in America and they all spoke very good English. They would pretend not to be Chinese. They would be an "American" group and they would never go into Chinatown. And the

Chinatown people would never go out because they could not communicate with the people outside. They feel very foreign and like outsiders. So I'm somewhere in between. I had to work there [in Chinatown] to earn money. I had to mix with all kinds of people.

SF: And in that respect, Jenny is somewhere in between at the end of the film. Although it's a happy ending, it's an open ending. She is living on Long Island, she is educated now, and she comes back to see Sam Pang ...

Cheung: But she doesn't deliberately come back. It's just by chance that they meet and you know they would never be able to get married, because they're so different. If I were to marry Sam Pang, I would be so angry because he cannot change, he has to gamble. He has these crazy friends, and they use foul language all the time. He doesn't like to go to Lincoln Center or to watch the kinds of movies I like. But we were very good friends. We only sort of lost contact in recent years.

SF: Tell me a little bit about the choice of Cherie Chung to play Jenny.

Cheung: For the female lead, actually, there were a lot of choices (unlike Chow Yun Fat who we believed was the only one). The character of Jennifer is just a common university girl — very spoiled in Hong Kong — but she slowly matures as she lives by herself. She learns how to cook and how to survive in a tough place. It's a growing up process for the woman. Cherie Chung is very good I think because she's also a bit "spoiled" (all female actresses are this way — well protected, worshipped). But then she has a kind of toughness about her.

SF: I believe the film is important because it moves us beyond the stereotypes of Chinese people that circulate in Hollywood films and in U.S. society.

Cheung: That's because the film is based on a real person and a real person is never a stereotype. If you truly base a film on a real person and you really have a feeling for him and you are careful with your character, then he will never be a stereotype. I think people who live in the film world move away from reality. You do not live in the real world. After awhile you live in the film world. You are surrounded by producers and film stars, and important people, so you lose touch. I was lucky because I lived in New York and I was all by myself then, and I got to know all of these interesting characters. I can re-create them to a certain extent in my films. That's why from time to time I stop making films and just try to live. If you do not live you cannot write. The kind of films that come out would be full of sound and fury — signifying nothing.

SF: How long were you in New York City alone?

Cheung: Maybe four or five years ... and I was really grateful to these guys because they did not really need me — a video tape sales girl. They could do it themselves — but I really needed a job. I had absolutely no money. I went to the shop every day around dinnertime because I knew they would go to dinner together, and they would invite all of their friends ... They liked to have big dinners with all kinds of friends. So I would kind of casually walk by the shop every evening. They would always invite me to dinner. After awhile they knew that I really needed a job. They pretended to be very casual about it, but they offered a job to me because they knew I needed the money.

SF: What about the question of gender? You've said elsewhere that you don't feel like you were discriminated against as a woman director. Do you stand by that?

Cheung: I have never felt a lot of discrimination against me as a woman and I grew up in a family where I was allowed to do anything because my father died when I was very small (in my teens). I was the eldest so I became the head of the family. My mother would always ask for my advice. I entered university of my own accord and I tried to do a lot of part-time jobs for school fees and things like that, so I've been very independent since I was very small and I supported my family as well. When I work I never differentiate between a man and a woman (although I like to behave like a woman because I like to wear pretty clothes) in that I relate like a woman and I think being a woman is nice. In fact, I'm very comfortable with my status as a woman because when you work you can work like a man or behave like whatever you like. I behave like myself. I never put up a front or try to pretend to be tougher than I am. In private life, I like to dress up and do whatever I like. I think if a woman sets herself free, then she is free. Maybe women consider being a director a tough job so a lot of women do not enter this business, especially in the East. It is a tough job, but I've been used to a tough life since I was very young.

Law: Come to think of it, by comparison to most other countries, there are more women directors in Hong Kong.

Cheung: And in China there are a lot of women directors too ...

SF: But when you first started directing, there weren't many women directors.

Cheung: Well you see, when I was small there were no women directors and all these men directors smoked cigars and wore dark glasses and wherever they went they had "chair boys" following them around the set and my mother would say, "Wow, look at the film world, all women in the film industry are hookers ..." So she was pretty disappointed when I decided to be a director. She liked to see me working in an office wearing high heels and skirts. That was her expectation for girls. She hated to see me running around in sneakers and pants.

SF: When did you know you wanted to become a director?

Cheung: Actually I never dreamed of becoming a film director. I wanted to be a dance hall girl because I like dancing — ballroom dancing. But then I went to study in England at Bristol University and BBC Bristol wanted to make a documentary about Hong Kong. They hired me as a production assistant and then I was exposed to the film world and to serious filmmakers. In filmmaking you have to be educated. You have to know a lot of things and I can use all of the knowledge I have of dancing, or sports, or whatever. I can use everything I've learned in my filmmaking. Most importantly, I don't have to sit in an office from nine to five.

SF: Alex, do people ever comment on your collaboration with Yuen-ting? Do you receive criticism because you choose to do movies that deal with real people and their feelings as opposed to kung-fu or action films?

Law: No, not really. I guess to do that — to collaborate with a woman — or to work on movies that are not really that mainstream … I don't know how to say this in English … You have to have a big heart — a heart that is big enough to accommodate the differences. That's how I feel about it.

SF: What brought you to filmmaking?

Law: It all happened when I was in high school. I used to sneak away from school and I'd be ambling around on the street with nothing much to do and somehow I'd always run into the school prefects. They were also running away from school. But they'd catch me and make me write the school rules three times. And it would take me three hours to write it just one time … So after awhile I figured out that if I ran away from school I had to find a place where nobody would see me. So I found this very quiet (and very cool in the summer) and very dark place where you see the laughter and the sorrows of life all by yourself with nobody there to hassle you. That's how I got into the habit of seeing movies and that's also how I fell in love with movies.

SF: There's a lot of discussion within feminist theory about cultural and generational difference. Some scholars argue that we are now in the "third wave" of feminism globally. Some critics argue that second-wave feminism was too angry, or perhaps anti-male. In some ways, Hong Kong has always been moving in that direction. Where do you see yourself in this debate?

Cheung: I've always been third wave. I have nothing against men. I like men. I have many men friends and if we are colleagues I respect them. I never pretend to be superior. I sometimes take advantage of being a woman. (Though if you have to make a film for three months, even if you are Nicole Kidman, people forget you are a woman.)

Law: After awhile on a shoot, nobody is a human being anyway. We're all reduced to being film animals.

Cheung: Nobody remembers who's a man and who's a woman and who's an E.T.! So third wave is definitely the thing. If you're a woman, you have to accept yourself as a woman and never pretend to be a man. At the beginning of my career, they said my voice was too weak. One time I pretended to shout a little bit and look a little more authoritative because back then nobody knew I was the director. At one point I said I will pretend to be more authoritative. And then after awhile I lost my voice. I decided maybe I should hire an Assistant Director who could shout at people with foul language — who has a bigger voice. So that would be OK. I don't have to pretend to be somebody I'm not. And from then on, I remained as I am. It's funny. In Hong Kong, they first came to know me as an American director, coming from New York because my first film was my thesis film. I made that all in New York with my classmates and friends. And I don't know why but it won me the best director's award at the Hong Kong film academy. So people who don't know me or where I come from — it's just like I descended upon them from America.

SF: Did that bother you?

Cheung: I'm ok with that when it works to my advantage because they would not question me anymore.

SF: Do you feel like you have become Americanized?

Cheung: No. I think in America I became more aware of my identity as a Chinese. In the eighties, people became more interested in Hong Kong because they all asked me questions about Hong Kong going back to China. It was a big thing back then — the historical background was important — and I suddenly discovered that I didn't know much about China. I was a bad student and I didn't study much Chinese history. So I read all of these books about China because although I'm a Chinese I studied in colonial Hong Kong and I knew more about the western than Chinese history. And so I wore a cheongsam, pretending to be very "oriental" and I became very aware of my identity as a Chinese. But then, of course, I understand the American way of thinking and I have a lot of American friends. I have nothing against the Americans. I'm happy with my advantages because I can communicate with all of the Americans and all of my friends, and then in China now I can speak more Mandarin and I have a lot of friends from mainland China too. So I would like to consider myself a cosmopolitan person.

SF: Alex, how about you?

Law: There are influences. I picked up some American habits (I never drank coffee before going there). I guess I've picked up more New York habits than American habits. To me, New York is very different from the rest of America.

SF: Did you have any of the same issues about identity that Yuen-ting did?

Law: Yes.

SF: How did they manifest themselves?

Law: I didn't react as strongly as she did and start wearing a Mao suit [laughter]. Also, when I was in high school, somehow I liked reading about Chinese history and culture a lot. I was the only student who did not take any Chinese courses in high school, which really drove my Chinese teacher crazy. He was so boring — which is why I ran away from school.

Cheung: Although some of my teachers were boring, I liked my English teachers. Actually, I picked up more English or American habits in Hong Kong than I did in England or America, because I listened to all of the Beatles songs, and I wore bell bottom pants and we had long hair, and I worshipped all things western (in the 70s). I formed my own folk song group and played the guitar, and sang all western songs. I can sing the whole book of folk songs in English. That was an important time.

Notes

Preface to *An Autumn's Tale*

1   Kwai-Cheung Lo, *Chinese Face/Off: The Transnational Popular Culture of Hong Kong* (Urbana: University of Illinois Press, 2005), 16.
2   Lisa Lowe, *Immigrant Acts: On Asian American Cultural Politics* (Durham: Duke University Press, 1996), 101.

Chapter 1   Introduction

1   Lisa Odham Stokes and Michael Hoover, *City on Fire: Hong Kong Cinema* (London: Verso, 1999), 28.
2   Stokes and Hoover, *City on Fire*, 106.
3   Stokes and Hoover, *City on Fire*, 28.
4   Ibid.
5   Stephen Teo, *Hong Kong Cinema: The Extra Dimensions* (London: British Film Institute Publishing, 1997), 188–189.

6   Esther M.K. Cheung and Chu Yiu-wai, *Between Home and World: A Reader in Hong Kong Cinema* (Hong Kong: Oxford University Press and Centre of Asian Studies, 2004), 417.

7   Cui Shuqin, "Stanley Kwan's *Center Stage*: The (Im)Possible Engagement Between Feminism and Postmodernism," in *Between Home and World,* 487–488.

8   Law Kar and Frank Ben, *Hong Kong Cinema: A Cross-Cultural View* (Oxford: Scarecrow Press, 2004), 293.

9   See Stephen Teo, *Hong Kong Cinema,* 160. The signing of the Joint Declaration in 1984 by Beijing and London fueled anxiety about Hong Kong's future and accelerated emigration, referred to as "the brain drain." Many of those who worked in the Hong Kong film industry were a part of this migration. Often, their experiences became material for diaspora films, as many of the New Wave/Second Wave directors were educated overseas.

10   Stephen Teo, *Hong Kong Cinema.*

11   Gina Marchetti, *From Tiananmen to Times Square: Transnational China and the Chinese Diaspora on Global Screens, 1989–1997* (Philadelphia: Temple University Press, 2006), 191.

12   Eliza W.Y. Lee, "Introduction," in Eliza W.Y. Lee, ed. *Gender and Change in Hong Kong: Globalization, Postcolonialism, and Chinese Patriarchy* (Hong Kong: Hong Kong University Press, 2003), 13.

13   Lisa Fischler, "Women's Activism During Hong Kong's Political Transition," in Eliza W.Y. Lee, ed., *Gender and Change in Hong Kong,* 69.

14   Gina Marchetti, "The Gender of GenerAsian X in Clara Law's Migration Trilogy," in Murray Pomerance, ed., *Ladies and Gentlemen, Boys and Girls: Gender in Film at the End of the Twentieth Century* (Albany: State University of New York Press, 2001), 71–87; Geetanjali Singh, "(Other)Feminisms — (Other) Values," in *Hecate: An Interdisciplinary Journal of Women's Liberation,* vol. 29, no. 2, (2003), 6; and Elaine Yee Lin Ho, "Women on the Edges of Hong Kong Modernity: The Films of Ann Hui," in Mayfair Mei-Hui Yang, ed., *Spaces of Their Own: Women's Public Sphere in Transnational China* (Minneapolis: University of Minnesota Press, 1999).

15   *The Status of Women and Girls in Hong Kong, 2006* (Hong Kong: The Women's Foundation, 2006).

16   Siumi Maria Tam, "Empowering Mobility: 'Astronaut' Women in Australia," in Eliza W.Y. Lee, ed., *Gender and Change in Hong Kong*, 198.

17   Yeeshan Chan, "Bringing Breasts into the Mainstream," in Laikwan Pang and Day Wong, eds., *Masculinities and Hong Kong Cinema* (Hong Kong: Hong Kong University Press, 2005), 187.

18   Jenny Kwok Wah Lau, "Besides Fists and Blood: Michael Hui and Cantonese Comedy," in Po Shek Fu and David Desser, eds., *The Cinema of Hong Kong: History, Arts, Identity* (Cambridge: Cambridge University Press, 2000), 160.

19   Peter X. Feng, *Screening Asian Americans* (New Brunswick: Rutgers University Press, 2002), 3.

20   Cheung and Chu, *Between Home and World*, 5. The authors note that, "Hong Kong tends to live in complicity with Hollywood as a 'marginal empire' — at least up to the mid-1990s before the decline of Hong Kong's film industry."

21   Cheung and Chu, *Between Home and World*, preface, xxiv.

22   See Law Kar and Frank Bren, *Hong Kong Cinema: A Cross-Cultural View* (Oxford: Scarecrow Press, 2004).

23   "Astronaut" is the term used to refer to people of Chinese descent who transited back and forth between Hong Kong and other global cities during this period in order to secure second homes and passports prior to the resumption of Chinese sovereignty.

Chapter 2 *An Autumn's Tale* as Transnational American Studies

1   Staci Ford, "Hong Kong Film Goes to the U.S.," *Hong Kong Film, Hollywood and the New Global Cinema: No Film Is an Island* (London: Routledge, 2007).

2   See Gina Marchetti, "Buying American, Consuming Hong Kong: Cultural Commerce, Fantasies of Identity, and the Cinema," in Fu, Po Shek, and David Desser, eds., *The Cinema of Hong Kong: History, Arts, Identity* (Cambridge: Cambridge University Press, 2000),

Chapter 13; and Ester C.M. Yau, "Introduction: Hong Kong Cinema in a Borderless World," in Esther C.M. Yau, ed., *At Full Speed: Hong Kong Cinema in a Borderless World* (Minneapolis: University of Minnesota Press, 2001), 2.

3   See Robert G. Lee, "Foreword," in Shilpa Dave, LeiLani Nishime, and Tasha G. Oren, eds., *East Main Street: Asian American Popular Culture* (New York: New York University Press, 2005), xiv.

4   Shelley Fisher Fishkin, "Crossroads of Cultures: The Transnational Turn in American Studies," Presidential Address to the American Studies Association, November 12, 2004, *American Quarterly*, March 2005, Vol. 57, No. 1, 20.

5   Henry Yu, "How Tiger Woods Lost His Stripes: Post-Nationalist American Studies as a History of Race, Migration, and the Commodification of Culture," in John Carlos Rowe, ed., *Post-Nationalist American Studies* (Berkeley: University of California Press, 2000), 224.

Chapter 4   *An Autumn's Tale*, Assimilation, and the American Dream

1   See Jennifer L. Hochschild, *Facing Up to the American Dream: Race, Class, and the State of the Nation* (Princeton: Princeton University Press, 1995), preface.

2   See Aihwa Ong, *Flexible Citizenship: The Cultural Logics of Transnationality* (Durham: Duke University Press, 1999).

3   The phrase "comforting narratives of liberal inclusion" is Victor Bascara's. Bascara is addressing the importance that Asian American texts play in helping to shed light on various forms of American imperialism. I would argue that Hong Kong films are, to a certain extent, both Asian American and Hong Kong cultural texts. As such, they help to unsettle myths and reveal imperialisms in both places. See Victor Bascara, *Model-Minority Imperialism* (Minneapolis: University of Minnesota Press, 2006, Introduction, xxv). The entire quotation reads, "These comforting narratives of liberal inclusion were predicated on the disappearance of the very U.S. imperialism that

emerged to manage Asian difference at the outset of the period of U.S. global hegemony that publisher Henry Luce, in early 1941, famously referred to as 'the American Century'."

4   Kwai-Cheung Lo, "Double Negations: Hong Kong Cultural Identity in Hollywood's Transnational Representations," in Cheung and Chu, *Between Home and World*, 67.

5   Ronald Takaki, *A Larger Memory: A History of Our Diversity with Voices* (Boston: Little, Brown and Company, 1998), 27.

6   Robert G. Lee, "Foreword," *East Main Street*, xiv. Bascara expresses similar critiques of the notion of multiculturalism in *Model Minority Imperialism*.

7   Gary Okihiro, *Margins and Mainstreams: Asians in American History and Culture* (Seattle: University of Washington Press, 1994), 155.

8   Gary Okihiro, *Common Ground: Reimagining American History* (Princeton: Princeton University Press, 2001), 126–127.

9   Carla Blank, *Rediscovering America: The Making of Multicultural America, 1900–2000* (New York: Three Rivers Press, 2003).

10 Yingchi Chu, *Hong Kong Cinema: Coloniser, Motherland and Self* (London: RoutledgeCurzon, 2003), 105.

11 Lisa Lowe, *Immigrant Acts*, preface.

12 Ibid.

13 Gina Marchetti, "Buying American, Consuming Hong Kong."

14 Chu, *Hong Kong Cinema,* xxi.

15 Chu, *Hong Kong Cinema*, 42.

16 Gary McDonogh and Cindy Wong, *Global Hong Kong* (New York: Routledge), 220.

17 Gina Marchetti, *From Tian'anmen to Times Square*, 6.

18 Interview with Mabel Cheung Yuen-ting and Alex Law, University of Hong Kong (HKU) Senior Common Room, 27 January 2007.

19 Although many scholars in Asian American and ethnic studies have addressed this subject, there is a succinct discussion of the origins and ongoing manifestation of model minority stereotypes (particularly as they connect to stereotypes of African Americans and Latinos) in Robert G. Lee's foreword to *East Main Street.*

20 Interview with Cheung and Law, HKU, 27 January 2007.

21 Stokes and Hoover, *City on Fire*, 153.

22 Julian Stringer, "Cultural Identity and Diaspora in Contemporary Hong Kong Cinema," in Darrell Y. Hamamoto and Sandra Liu, eds., *Countervisions: Asian American Film Criticism* (Philadelphia: Temple University Press), 303–304.

23 Stringer, "Cultural Identity and Diaspora," 303.

24 Ibid.

25 Kwai-Cheung Lo, "Transnationalization of the Local in Hong Kong Cinema of the 1990s," in Esther C.M. Yau, ed., *At Full Speed: Hong Kong Cinema in a Borderless World* (Minneapolis: University of Minnesota Press, 2001), 264.

26 Stringer, "Cultural Identity and Diaspora," 306–307.

27 Interview with Cheung and Law, HKU, 26 June 2006. See Appendix.

28 Lisa Lowe, *Immigrant Acts,* 6.

29 Gina Marchetti, "Buying American, Consuming Hong Kong," 308–309.

30 Comments made by an anonymous reader offered this interpretation of the film's ending — one that I agree with but cannot claim as my own originally.

31 Interview with Cheung and Law, HKU, 27 January 2007.

32 The "Here's Looking at You, Kid" moniker was applied to some of our earliest courses in American studies at the University of Hong Kong. Geetanjali Singh deserves credit for using the famous *Casablanca* line in this context, and for originating a course on Asian views of the U.S.

33 Interview with Cheung and Law, HKU, 27 January 2007.

Chapter 5   A Tale of Two Cities: New York in *An Autumn's Tale*

1 Yingchi Chu, *Hong Kong Cinema: Coloniser, Motherland and Self.* (London: RoutledgeCurzon, 2003), 106–107.

2 Interview with Mabel Cheung Yuen-ting and Alex Law, HKU Senior Common Room, 27 January 2007.

3 Ibid.

4 Ibid.

5 Ibid.

6   Kwai-Cheung Lo, *Chinese Face/Off*, 113–114.
7   Gina Marchetti, *From Tian'anmen to Times Square*, 175.
8   Interview with Cheung and Law, HKU, 26 June 2006.
9   Julian Stringer, "Cultural Identity and Diaspora," 302.
10   Stringer, "Cultural Identity," 305.
11   Interview with Cheung and Law, HKU, 26 June 2006.
12   Interview with Cheung and Law, HKU, 27 January 2007.
13   Marchetti, *From Tian'anmen to Times Square*, 9.
14   Stringer, "Cultural Identity," 308.

Chapter 6   Reconfiguring Gender in Diaspora

1   Dialogue from *Farewell China* as quoted in Stokes and Hoover, *City on Fire*, 154.
2   Gina Marchetti, "Transnational Exchanges, Questions of Culture, and Global Cinema: Defining the Dynamics of Changing Relationships," in Yau, *At Full Speed*, 258.
3   Day Wong, "Women's Reception of Mainstream Hong Kong Cinema," in Laikwan Pang and Day Wong, eds., *Masculinities and Hong Kong Cinema* (Hong Kong: Hong Kong University Press, 2005), 251.
4   Cheung and Ku in Cheung and Chu, *Between Home and World*.
5   See discussion of the Clarence Thomas hearings in Carla Blank, *Rediscovering America: The Making of Multicultural America, 1900–2000* (New York: Three Rivers Press, 2003), 391. On the 1980s and backlash, see Susan Faludi, *Backlash: The Undeclared War Against American Women*. (New York: Crown, 1991).
6   Geetanjali Singh, *(Other) Feminisms, Other Values*.
7   Evelyn G.H. Ng and Catherine W. Ng, "Single Working Women in Hong Kong: A Case of Normal Deviance?" Paper presented at the "Doing Families" symposium, The University of Hong Kong, 11 November 2006.
8   Suzanna Danuta Walters, "Sex, Text, and Context: (In) Between Feminism and Cultural Studies," in Myra Marx Ferree, Judith Lorber, and Beth B. Hess, *Revisioning Gender* (Thousand Oaks, CA: Sage Publications, 1999), 229.

9   Christine So, "'A Woman is Nothing:' Valuing the Modern Chinese Woman's Epic Journey to the West," in *East Main Street,* 139.

10   Interview with Mabel Cheung Yuen-ting, HKU, 26 June 2006.

11   Jeff Yang, *Once Upon a Time in China: A Guide to Hong Kong, Taiwanese, and Mainland Chinese Cinema* (New York: Atria Books), 86. See also Stefan Hammond, *Hollywood East: Hong Kong Movies and the People Who Make Them.* (Chicago: Contemporary Books, 2000), 187.

12   Julian Stringer, "Your Tender Smiles Give Me Strength: Paradigms of Masculinity in John Woo's *A Better Tomorrow* and *The Killer*," in *Between Home and World,* 449–450.

13   Stringer, "Your Tender Smiles," 453.

14   Sheridan Prasso, *The Asian Mystique: Dragon Ladies, Geisha Girls, and Our Fantasies of the Exotic Orient* (New York: Public Affairs, 2005), 103.

15   Laikwan Pang, "Introduction: The Diversity of Masculinities in Hong Kong Cinema," in Laikwan Pang and Day Wong, eds., *Masculinities and Hong Kong Cinema*, 8.

16   Susan Jeffords, *Hard Bodies: Hollywood Masculinity in the Reagan Era* (New Brunswick: Rutgers University Press, 1994), 52–53.

17   Kwai-Cheung Lo, *Chinese Face/Off*, 160.

18   Kam Louie, *Theorising Chinese Masculinity: Society and Gender in China* (Cambridge: Cambridge University Press, 2002), 142.

19   Robert G. Lee, *East Main Street*, "Foreword," xiii.

20   King-Kok Cheung, "The Woman Warrior Versus the Chinaman Pacific: Must a Chinese American Critic Choose Between Feminism and Heroism?" in Jean Yu-wen Shen Wu and Min Song, eds., *Asian American Studies: A Reader* (New Brunswick: Rutgers University Press), 308.

21   Louie, *Theorizing Chinese Masculinity*, 4–6.

22   Stringer, "Cultural Identity and Diaspora," 308.

23   King-Kok Cheung, "The Woman Warrior Versus the Chinaman Pacific," 308.

24   Wai-Kit Choi, "Post-Fordist Production and the Re-appropriation of Hong Kong Masculinity," in Pang and Wong, eds. *Masculinities and Hong Kong Cinema*, 211.

Chapter 7   Conclusion

1   Chris Yeung, "Former broadcasting chief steps into row over TV rulings, " *South China Morning Post,* 28 January 2007.
2   Interview with Mabel Cheung Yuen-ting and Alex Law, HKU Senior Common Room, 27 January 2007.
3   Chris Yeung, "Cod morality gives the lie to 'world-class HK' tag," in "Chris Yeung at Large," *South China Morning Post,* 28 January 2007.

Credits

An Autumn's Tale (秋天的童話)

Hong Kong 1987

Director
Mabel Cheung Yuen-ting

Screenplay
Alex Law

Production Supervisor
Linda Kuk

Original Music
Lowell Lo

Art Directors
Christy Addis
Yank Wong

Editor
Cheong Kwok-kuen

Executive Producer
Dickson Poon

Producer
John Sham

Associate Producer
Winnie Yu

Director of Photography
James Hayman

Additional Photography
David Chung

Production
D&B Films

Distributors
Fortune Star/Star TV

Cast
Chow Yun Fat (周潤發)   as Figgy/Samuel Pang (船頭尺)
Cherie Chung (鍾楚紅)   as Jenny (李琪/十三妹)
Danny Chan (陳百強)   as Vincent
Gigi Wong (黃淑儀)   as Mrs. Sherwood
Brenda Lo (盧業瑂)   as May-chu May

Filmographies

Mabel Cheung Yuen-ting
Director/Producer/Writer

Stage

2005   Directed the musical "Song of Light and Shadow" commemorating the 100th anniversary of movie making in China

Films

2003   Directed *TRACES OF A DRAGON*
— a documentary about Jackie Chan and his family.
Opening film for the Berlin Film Festival Panorama Documentary Series, 2003
Nominated for Best Documentary Award (2003) at the Taiwan Golden Horse Awards

2001   Directed *BEIJING ROCKS*
— a film about the new generation and the rock and roll scene in Beijing.

Nominated for five Hong Kong Film Awards (2002), including Best Picture

1998   Directed *CITY OF GLASS*
Winner of 5 Golden Horse Awards in Taiwan (1998), including Best Picture (Audience's Choice) and Best Screenplay, Most Outstanding Film and Most Outstanding Director of 1999 (Hong Kong Film Directors' Guild)

1997   Directed *THE SOONG SISTERS*
Winner of Best Picture, Golden Rooster Awards for Co-production, China (1997)
Winner of 3 Golden Horse Awards in Taiwan (1997)
Winner of 6 Hong Kong Film Awards (1998), including Best Actress

1993   Produced the martial arts film *THE MOON WARRIORS*

1991   Produced and co-wrote Alex Law's comedy *NOW YOU SEE LOVE, NOW YOU DON'T*

1989   Directed *EIGHT TAELS OF GOLD*
Named one of the 10 Best Films of the Year (1989) by the Hong Kong Film Academy

1988   Executive produced and co-wrote Alex Law's *PAINTED FACES*
Winner of 7 Golden Horse Awards in Taiwan (1998), including Best Picture, Best Director and Best Screenplay
Winner of the Silver Hugo Award for Best First Feature at the 25th Chicago International Film Festival (1989)

1987   Directed *AN AUTUMN'S TALE*
Winner of 5 Hong Kong Film Awards (1987), including Best Picture, Best Screenplay and Best Actor
Winner of Best Picture and Best Screenplay at the Hong Kong Film Directors' Choice (1987)
Named one of the Ten Classics of the Century in Hong Kong (2000)

1985   Directed *THE ILLEGAL IMMIGRANT*
— first feature film and NYU thesis film
Winner of Best Director at the Hong Kong Film Awards (1985)
Winner of the Special Jury Award at the 30th Asia Pacific Film
Festival (1985)

Education

M.F.A. in Film Production, New York University Graduate Film School
Advanced Diploma in Drama and Visual Arts, Bristol University
B.A. in English Literature and Psychology at the University of Hong Kong

Alex Law
Producer / Director / Writer / Lyricist

Stage

2006   Artistic Director, Playwright and Lyricist for SONG OF LIGHT
AND SHADOW, a multi-media musical commemorating the
100th anniversary of the birth of Chinese Cinema.

Film

2005–   Pre-production for *THE LEGEND OF AH TOY*
— an epic story of the early Chinese immigrants in America.

2003   Produced *TRACES OF A DRAGON*
— a documentary on Jackie Chan and his family.
Opening film for the Berlin Film Festival Panorama Documentary
Series, 2003

2002   Produced and wrote *BEIJING ROCKS*
— a film about China's new generation and the underground rock
and roll scene in Beijing.
Nominated for 5 Hong Kong Film Awards (2002), including Best
Picture

1998   Produced and wrote *CITY OF GLASS*
Winner of 5 Golden Horse Awards in Taiwan (1998), including Best Picture (Audience's Choice) and Best Screenplay
Most Outstanding Film and Most Outstanding Director of 1999 (Hong Kong Film Directors' Guild)

1997   Produced and wrote *THE SOONG SISTERS*
Winner of Best Picture, Golden Rooster Awards for Co-production, China (1997)
Winner of 3 Golden Horse Awards in Taiwan (1997)
Winner of 6 Hong Kong Film Awards (1998), including Best Actress

1994   Produced and wrote the martial arts film *THE MOON WARRIORS*

1992   Wrote and directed *NOW YOU SEE LOVE, NOW YOU DON'T*

1990   Produced and wrote *EIGHT TAELS OF GOLD*
Named one of the Ten Best Films of the Year (1989) by the Hong Kong Film Academy

1988   Wrote and directed *PAINTED FACES*
Winner of 7 Golden Horse Awards in Taiwan (1998), including Best Picture, Best Director and Best Screenplay
Winner of the Silver Hugo Award for Best First Feature at the 25th Chicago International Film Festival (1989)

1987   Produced and wrote *AN AUTUMN'S TALE*
Winner of 5 Hong Kong Film Awards (1987), including Best Picture, Best Screenplay and Best Actor
Winner of Best Picture and Best Screenplay at the Hong Kong Film Directors' Choice Awards (1987)
Named one of the Ten Classics of the Century in Hong Kong (2000)

1985   Produced and wrote *THE ILLEGAL IMMIGRANT*
Winner of the Special Jury Award at the 30th Asia Pacific Film Festival (1985)

1984   Awarded Best Cinematographer for *BLUE CHRISTMAS* in the 1984 New York University Film Festival

Television

1978–81 Produced and directed over 20 drama programs at Radio/ Television Hong Kong, including:
  GOODBYE, SUZIE WONG
  GETHSEMANE
  CASTLE OF SAND
  SUFFER THE LITTLE CHILDREN
  FAREWELL MY CONCUBINE

Education

M.F.A. in Film Production, New York University Graduate Film School
B.A. in Chinese and English Literature at the University of Hong Kong

Bibliography

Abbas, Ackbar, *Hong Kong: Culture and the Politics of Disappearance* (Hong Kong/Minneapolis: Hong Kong University/University of Minnesota Press, 1997).

Ahluwalia, Sanjam, "Rethinking Boundaries: Feminisms and (Inter) Nationalism in Early-Twentieth-Century India," *Journal of Women's History,* Vol. 14, No. 4, Winter 2003.

Bascara, Victor, *Model Minority Imperialism* (Minneapolis: University of Minnesota Press, 2006).

Bender, Thomas, *A Nation Among Nations: America's Place in World History* (New York: Hill & Wang, 2006).

Berry, Chris, and Mary Farquhar, *China on Screen: Cinema and Nation* (Hong Kong: Hong Kong University Press, 2006).

Bordwell, David, *Planet Hong Kong: Popular Cinema and the Art of Entertainment* (Cambridge: Harvard University Press, 2000).

Browne, Nick, Paul G. Pickowicz, Vivian Sobchack, and Esther Yau, *New Chinese Cinemas: Forms, Identities, Politics.* (Cambridge: Cambridge University Press, 1994).

Chan, Anita Kit-wa, and Wong Wai-ling, *Gendering Hong Kong,* (Hong Kong: Oxford University Press, 2004).

Cheung, Esther M.K., and Chu Yiu-wai, *Between Home and World: A Reader in Hong Kong Cinema* (Oxford: Oxford University Press and Hong Kong: Centre for Asian Studies, University of Hong Kong, 2004).

Cheung, King-Kok, "The Woman Warrior Versus the Chinaman Pacific: Must a Chinese American Critic Choose Between Feminism and Heroism?" *Asian American Studies: A Reader,* Jean Yu-wen Shen Wu and Min Song, eds., (New Brunswick: Rutgers University Press, 2000).

Chow, Rey, "Against the Lures of Diaspora: Minority Discourse, Chinese Women, and Intellectual Hegemony," *Gender and Sexuality in Twentieth-Century Chinese Literature and Society*, Tonglin Lu, ed., (Albany: State University Press of New York, 1993).

_____, *Primitive Passions: Visuality, Sexuality, Ethnography, and Contemporary Chinese Cinema* (New York: Columbia University Press, 1995).

Chu, Patricia P., *Assimilating Asians: Gendered Strategies of Authorship in Asian America* (Durham: Duke University Press, 2000).

Chung, Ricky, "Green Idol: Cherie Chung," *South China Morning Post,* 12 March 2006.

Dannen, Fredric, and Barry Long, *Hong Kong Babylon: An Insider's Guide to the Hollywood of the East* (New York: Hyperion, 1997).

Dave, Shilpa, LeiLani Nishime, and Tasha G. Oren, *East Main Street: Asian American Popular Culture* (New York: NYU Press, 2005).

Disch, Estelle, ed., *Reconstructing Gender: A Multicultural Anthology* (Mountain View: Mayfield, 1997.)

Faure, David, ed., *Hong Kong: A Reader in Social History* (Oxford: Oxford University Press, 2003).

Feng, Peter X., *Identities in Motion: Asian American Film and Video* (Durham: Duke University Press, 2002).

_____, ed., *Screening Asian Americans* (New Brusnswick: Rutgers University Press, 2002).

Ferree, Myra Marx, Judith Lorber, and Beth B. Hess, eds., *Revisioning Gender* (Thousand Oaks: Sage, 1999).

Fishkin, Shelly Fisher, "Crossroads of Cultures: The Transnational Turn in American Studies," Presidential Address to the American Studies Association, November 12, 2004, *American Quarterly,* March 2005, Vol. 57, No. 1, 17–57.

Ford, Staci, "Claiming the Space: Fictionalising Feminism in Xu Xi's 1990s Hong Kong Novels," *Lilith: A Feminist History Journal*, No. 14, 2005, 52–64.

_____. "Hong Kong Film Goes to America," Gina Marchetti and Tan See Kam, eds., *Hong Kong Film, Hollywood and the New Global Cinema: No Film Is an Island* (London: Routledge, 2007).

Fu, Po Shek, and David Desser, eds., *The Cinema of Hong Kong: History, Arts, Identity* (Cambridge: Cambridge University Press, 2000).

Gao, Ge, and Stella Ting-Toomey, *Communicating Effectively with the Chinese* (Thousand Oaks, CA: Sage, 1998).

Goh, Robbie B.H., and Shawn Wong, *Asian Diasporas: Cultures, Identities, Representations* (Hong Kong: Hong Kong University Press, 2004).

Hamamoto, Darrell Y., and Sandra Liu, eds., *Countervisions: Asian American Film Criticism* (Philadelphia: Temple University Press, 2000).

Hamilton, Gary G., ed., *Cosmopolitan Capitalists: Hong Kong and the Chinese Diaspora at the End of the Twentieth Century* (Seattle: University of Washington Press, 1999).

Hammond, Stefan, *Hollywood East: Hong Kong Movies and the People Who Make Them* (Chicago: Contemporary Books, 2000).

Ho, Elaine Yee Lin, "Women on the Edges of Hong Kong Modernity: The Films of Ann Hui," Mayfair Mei-Hui Yang, ed., *Spaces of Their Own: Women's Public Sphere in Transnational China* (Minneapolis: University of Minnesota Press, 1999).

Hochschild, Jennifer L., *Facing Up to the American Dream: Race, Class, and the Soul of the Nation* (Princeton: Princeton University Press, 1995).

Hong Kong Cinema Retrospective: Fifty Years of Electric Shadows: The 21st Hong Kong *International Film Festival* (Hong Kong: The Urban Council of Hong Kong, 1997).

Hong Kong Cinema, '79–'89: The 24th International Hong Kong Film Festival (Hong Kong: Leisure and Cultural Services Department, 2001).

Jeffords, Susan, *Hard Bodies: Hollywood Masculinity in the Reagan Era* (New Brunswick: Rutgers University Press, 1994).

Kaplan, Amy, and Donald E. Pease, eds., *Cultures of United States Imperialism* (Durham: Duke University Press, 1993).

Kazin, Michael, and Joseph A. McCartin, eds., *Americanism: New Perspectives on the History of an Ideal* (Chapel Hill: The University of North Carolina Press, 2006)

Law, Kar, and Frank Bren, *Hong Kong Cinema: A Cross-Cultural View* (Lanham: Scarecrow Press, 2004).

Lee, Eliza W.Y., ed., *Gender and Change in Hong Kong: Globalization, Postcolonialism, and Chinese Patriarchy* (Hong Kong: Hong Kong University Press, 2003).

Li, Chenyang, ed., *The Sage and the Second Sex: Confucianism, Ethics, and Gender* (Chicago: Open Court, 2000).

Lo, Kwai-Cheung, *Chinese Face/Off: The Transnational Popular Culture of Hong Kong* (Urbana: University of Illinois Press, 2005).

Locher-Scholten, Elsbeth, "Morals, Harmony, and National Identity: 'Companionate Feminism' in Colonial Indonesia in the 1930s," *Journal of Women's History: Revising the Experiences of Colonized Women Beyond Binaries,* Claire C. Robertson and Nupur Chaudhuri, eds., Winter 2003, Vol. 14, No. 4.

Lorber, Judith, and Beth B. Hess, *Revisioning Gender* (Thousand Oaks, CA: Sage Publications, 1999).

Louie, Kam, *Theorizing Chinese Masculinity: Society and Gender in China* (Cambridge: Cambridge University Press, 2002).

Lowe, Lisa, *Immigrant Acts: On Asian American Cultural Politics* (Durham: Duke University Press, 1996).

Lu, Sheldon Hsiao-peng, ed., *Transnational Chinese Cinemas: Identity, Nationhood, Gender* (Honolulu: University of Hawai'i Press, 1997).

Marchetti, Gina, "Buying American, Consuming Hong Kong: Cultural Commerce, Fantasies of Identity, and the Cinema," in Fu, Po Shek, and David Desser, eds., *The Cinema of Hong Kong: History, Arts, Identity* (Cambridge: Cambridge University Press, 2000), Chapter 13.

_____, *From Tian'anmen to Times Square: Transnational China and the Chinese Diaspora on Global Screens, 1989–1997* (Philadelphia: Temple University Press, 2006).

_____, "The Gender of GenerAsian X in Clara Law's Migration Trilogy," in Murray Pomerance, ed., *Ladies and Gentlemen, Boys and Girls: Gender in Film at the End of the Twentieth Century* (Albany: State University of New York Press, 2001), 71–87.

_____, *Romance and the "Yellow Peril": Race, Sex and Discursive Strategies in Hollywood Fiction* (Berkeley: University of California Press, 1993).

McDonogh, Gary, and Cindy Wong, *Global Hong Kong* (New York: Routledge, 2005).

Morris, Meaghan, Siu Leung Li, and Stephen Chan Ching-kiu, eds., *Hong Kong Connections: Transnational Imagination in Action Cinema* (Durham: Duke University Press, 2005).

Narayan, Uma, and Sandra Harding, eds., *Decentering the Center: Philosophy for a Multicultural, Postcolonial, and Feminist World* (Bloomington: Indiana University Press, 2000).

Ng, Catherine W. and Evelyn G.H. Ng, "Hong Kong Single Working Women's Pragmatic Negotiation of Work and Personal Space," in *Anthropology of Work Review*, Vol. XXV, Nos. 1–2, 8–14.

Okihiro, Gary Y., *The Columbia Guide to Asian American History* (New York: Columbia University Press, 2001).

_____, *Common Ground: Reimagining American History* (Princeton: Princeton University Press, 2001).

_____, *Margins and Mainstreams: Asians in American History and Culture* (Seattle: University of Washington Press, 1994).

Ong, Aihwa, *Flexible Citizenship: The Cultural Logics of Transnationality* (Durham: Duke University Press, 1999).

Ong, Jin Hui, Chan Kwok Bun, and Chew Soon Beng, *Crossing Borders: Transmigration in Asia Pacific* (Singapore: Prentice Hall, 1995).

Pang, Laikwan and Day Wong, *Masculinities and Hong Kong Cinema* (Hong Kong: Hong Kong University Press, 2005).

Prasso, Sheridan, *The Asian Mystique: Dragon Ladies, Geisha Girls, and Our Fantasies of the Exotic Orient* (New York: Public Affairs, 2005).

Rowe, John Carlos, ed., *Post-Nationalist American Studies* (Berkeley: University of California Press, 2000).

Signs: Journal of Women in Culture and Society, Special Issue: Film Feminisms, Vol. 30, No. 1, Autumn 2004.

Singh, Geetanjali, "(Other) Feminisms — (Other) Values," *Hecate: An Interdisciplinary Journal of Women's Liberation*, Vol. 29, No. 2, (2003).

Stokes, Lisa Odham, and Michael Hoover, *City on Fire: Hong Kong Cinema* (London: Verso, 1999).

Takaki, Ronald, *A Larger Memory: A History of Our Diversity, with Voices* (Boston: Little, Brown and Company, 1998).

Tam, Kwok-kan and Wimal Dissanayake, *New Chinese Cinema* (Oxford: Oxford University Press, 1998).

Teo, Stephen, *Hong Kong Cinema: The Extra Dimensions* (London: British Film Institute Publishing, 1997).

Thurer, Shari L., *The End of Gender: A Psychological Autopsy* (New York: Routledge, 2005).

Wang, Gungwu, ed., *Global History and Migrations* (Boulder: Westview Press, 1997).

Wesoky, Sharon, *Chinese Feminism Faces Globalization* (New York: Routledge, 2002).

Wing Kai Chiu and Tai Lok Lui, eds., *The Dynamics of Social Movement in Hong Kong* (Hong Kong: Hong Kong University Press, 2000).

Wong, K. Scott, "The Transformation of Culture: Three Chinese Views of America," *American Quarterly, Vol.* 48 (June 1996), 201–32.

Wu, Frank H., *Yellow: Race in America Beyond Black and White* (New York: Basic Books, 2002).

Yang, Jeff, *Once Upon a Time in China: A Guide to Hong Kong, Taiwanese, and Mainland Chinese Cinema* (New York: Atria Books, 2003).

Yau Ching, *Filming Margins: Tang Shu Shuen: A Forgotten Hong Kong Woman Director* (Hong Kong: Hong Kong University Press, 2004).

Yau, Esther C.M., ed., *At Full Speed: Hong Kong Cinema in a Borderless World* (Minneapolis: University of Minnesota Press, 2001).

Yuval-Davis, Nira, *Gender and Nation* (London: Sage, 1997).